DESTINY'S CHILDREN

'This book will make you cry, make you angry and make you pray. It is a prophetic call from a pastoral heart challenging young and old to grasp, as Anita says, that "their personal story has a unique role in God's grand story". Birthed out of God's journeying with Anita through her own tragedies and triumphs, this biblically grounded, culturally connected book means business, and will lead to action—bent kness, broken hearts, burning witnesses.'

Simon Ponsonby, author of More

'The moment I started to read this book it warmed my heart and challenged my soul.'

Dianne Parsons

'Anita explores the subject of destiny in a most thought-provoking and moving way. This book will both grip and inspire you.'

Mary Pytches

Dedication

In memory of my father, Lewis,
and
for Hannah, Alice, Jack and Jemimah.

Destiny's Children

ANITA CLEVERLY

 LIFE JOURNEY®

Bringing Home the Message for Life

KINGSWAY COMMUNICATIONS LTD, EASTBOURNE, ENGLAND

COOK COMMUNICATIONS MINISTRIES

COLORADO SPRINGS • PARIS, ONTARIO

Life Journey is an imprint of
KINGSWAY COMMUNICATIONS LTD
Lottbridge Drove, Eastbourne BN23 6NT, England.
Email: books@kingsway.co.uk

Printed in the USA

Contents

Preface

For over 20 years this book has been in gestation. The seed of it was planted with the death of our son Samuel at the age of two-and-a-half months in 1982. About two years later, when the grief was subsiding, though not yet fully done, I felt the first stirrings of the desire to communicate the story, not for the sake of it, but because subsequent to Samuel's death I had met many parents grieving without hope. Surely, I reasoned, we who had a hope in the face of death should share it with those who were walking in a terrible darkness.

The years have passed, and as I write, Samuel's younger brother Jack is standing on the threshold of adult life as he approaches the end of his university years. We await the birth of our first grandchild with awe and excitement.

Just as a child in the womb develops in a mysterious and marvellous way, imperceptibly yet unquestionably, so this book has distinctly evolved from the days of those first stirrings. The trigger of it may be Samuel, and much of what I write is seen through the lens of his brief life, but my aim is to show how to reconcile life's inevitable trials with an unwavering determination to find and embrace our God-given destinies. I write for you whether you are an adult seeking for yourself, a parent seeking for a child, a child seeking for a parent, a young person or a student. Whoever you are, and whatever your age, you have a destiny.

As the world grows darker, so the tide of longing to live, work and love in a meaningful way that benefits humanity swells in the hearts of many; but the distractions and seductions are multiple and overpowering. We will all forever remember that different and terrible tide, the Boxing Day tsunami of 2004 that brutally cut short tens of thousands of lives around the coasts of the Indian Ocean. Every one of those lives had a destiny and was created for a noble purpose. It took time for us to assimilate the implications of what some called the world's greatest natural disaster. The power of nature and the fragility of man could not have been more graphically illustrated than in this event. If the condition of so many countries can be completely changed in a matter of seconds, would we not be wise to pursue our destiny for all we are worth?

We live in darkening days, and none of us knows how many of those days remain to us. The greater the chaos and confusion that threaten to engulf us, the greater should be our passion to search out meaning and truth.

I lived in inner-city Paris for ten years from 1992–2002. My family's stamping ground was the 19th and 20th arrondissements, a multicultural part of the city, well off the beaten track of the tourist. Traditionally host to the latest wave of refugees from around the world, poverty of all kinds was painfully visible, not the least of these poverty of spirit. Every day we rubbed shoulders with the broken-hearted, those who mourned and those who were clothed in a spirit of despair. My sense of unease and helplessness in the face of the anguished multitudes of sheep without a shepherd led me to reflect about the themes of this book, feeling acutely as I did my inadequacy in the face of such overwhelming human misery.

What was it that enabled us to ride the storm of Samuel's death and find the healing by degrees that today finds us established in the work of building a local church now in the challenging atmosphere of Oxford's ivory towers, and formerly in the frenetic, dirty, and vibrant part of Paris that was our home for ten years? I want to answer that question through some words of C. S. Lewis in *The Silver Chair.*

> Crying is all right in its way while it lasts. But you have to stop sooner or later, and then you still have to decide what to do. When Jill stopped, she found she was dreadfully thirsty. . .The birds had ceased singing and there was perfect silence except for one small, persistent sound, which seemed to come from a good distance away. She listened carefully, and felt almost sure it was the sound of running water.

She follows the sound until,

> she came to an open glade and saw the stream, bright as glass, running across the turf a stone's throw away from her. But although the sight of the water made her feel ten times thirstier than before, she didn't rush forward and drink. She stood as still as if she'd been turned into stone. And she had a very good reason; just on this side of the stream lay the lion.

Paralysed by fear, Jill deliberates for a long moment, while the thirst intensifies until,

> she almost felt she would not mind being eaten by the lion if only she could be sure of getting a mouthful of water first.

'If you're thirsty, you may drink.'. . .the voice was not like a man's. It was deeper, wilder and stronger. . .It did not make her any less frightened than she had been before, but it made her frightened in rather a different way.

'Are you not thirsty?' said the Lion.

'I'm dying of thirst,' said Jill.

'Then drink,' said the Lion.

'May I—could I—would you mind going away while I do?' said Jill. . . 'Will you promise not to—do anything to me, if I do come?'

'I make no promise,' said the Lion.

Jill was so thirsty now that, without noticing it, she had come a step nearer.

'Do you eat girls?' she said.

'I have swallowed up girls and boys, women and men, kings and emperors, cities and realms,' said the Lion. It didn't say this as if it were boasting, nor as if it were sorry, nor as if it were angry. It just said it.

'I daren't come and drink,' said Jill.

'Then you will die of thirst,' said the Lion.

'Oh dear!' said Jill, coming another step nearer. 'I suppose I must go and look for another stream then.'

'There is no other stream,' said the Lion.

It was by drinking from the only stream when I was dying of thirst that I found out how to get up and what to do next.

My hope is that this book will bring consolation to you if you are fighting for breath after tragedy, that it will explain things that have long been a source of pain for you, or that it will kickstart you into a diligent pursuit of God and the discovery—or recovery—of your destiny. Lastly, I pray that if you have never tasted this water, 'the coldest, most refreshing water she had ever tasted,' that, 'quenches your thirst at once,' then you will taste it here and be introduced to the wonders of knowing Jesus Christ, the most remarkable person ever to walk on this earth.

It is the tale of an ordinary family, and yet any life that is touched by Jesus is transformed, like those of Peter, James and John who saw him transfigured. For a brief moment they saw into heaven and their lives were never the same again.

My prayer is that together we will glimpse heaven and find, each according to his need and cry, the touch of Jesus, which will mean that we shall never be quite the same again.

Anita Cleverly
Oxford, January 2005

Acknowledgements

I've known I wanted to be a writer for as long as I can remember—old exercise books full of short stories and a file full of poems bear witness to that—but I never imagined what a rollercoaster experience actually writing a real book would be! Doubting castles and sloughs of despond have abounded, but so have moments of breakthrough and sheer exhilaration.

Right from the starting block there have been wonderful people who have held my hand, picked me up when I've fallen, cheered me on and given very constructive criticism. Other wonderful people have contributed to the extensive pedestrian work that is involved in the crafting of a book. I thank every one of them.

First, thank you to Richard Herkes of Kingsway for taking the risk of believing that I could do this! Thank you for helpful comments and suggestions. Thank you to Carolyn Owen, also of Kingsway, for your calm, consistent and wise advice.

I first met Michele Guinness many years ago and have never ceased to be an admirer of her amazing abilities as an author as well as her abilities as a woman, speaker, mother, organiser of the NHS for the whole of the north west, her pint-sized shape, her brilliant flair for dressing and her fabulous humour. . .and I don't imagine for a moment that my list is exhaustive. Michele kindly read the embryonic manuscript in a train on her way to London, and made insightful and creative suggestions, for which I am grateful. Thank you, Michele.

Mary Pytches has been a role model for me for very many years. She has been unswervingly encouraging every time I have ventured to articulate my dream of writing a book, and at moments of darkness and discouragement, her steady voice and down to earth words have helped me to persevere. Her own books have been a great inspiration to me. Thank you, Mary.

I owe a debt of gratitude to some beloved friends whose stories are in the book. Firstly to Margaret Watts, a Lydia national team member, and her husband Colin, who kindly gave me permission to write about their son Stephen; to dear friends Dan and Suzie (not their real names) who have allowed me to include the story of their tiny daughter; it has been a privilege to put words around something so deep. And to my dear co-missionary in France, Angela Beise, who generously gave me permission to include her piece of writing about her son Michael. You are all inestimably precious to me.

Thank you to Cathryn Hall of Viva Networks, our lodger-daughter, who ploughed through the manuscript on a long-haul flight to Indonesia, and made helpful corrections and suggestions; to Pete Wigley, the ultimate administrator, who organised the final version of the manuscript with im-maculate calm in a very short time and with very little warning; and to my incomparable PA, Lois Heris, who has been unfailingly encouraging, enthusiastic and patient: you are all the most fantastic children of destiny, and I am standing on the sidelines on tiptoe to see how God works out those destinies.

Thank you to James and Gill Kelly for lending us your fabulous flat, where we have hidden away to write at a window looking out over the stunning Pembrokeshire coast, and walked the windy beach to untangle our thoughts.

Without the demonstration of friendship given to us at the time of Samuel's death, and ever since, I doubt I could have undertaken such a project. Stuart and Celia, you embody for us the meaning of friendship. Thank you for the laughter, the tears, the prayers, the haven of your home on many occasions as well as that early walk together through the valley of the shadow of death. Thank you for the challenges to my woolly thinking, the championing of my destiny and the chilling of the white wine!

Thank you to my sister Miranda and brother-in law Peter Harris, founders of Arocha International. Together you have been a constant inspiration and source of energy. You keep us from atrophy! Your friendship is treasured.

I want to pay tribute to my parents, Lewis and Betty Dodd, for their lifelong belief in me and unfailing encouragement; and for the writing gene that I believe I have inherited from Dad. Likewise my thanks go to my four surviving children for being the people they are. . .true children of destiny. I am so proud of you all. Thank you for believing that your mum could do this!

Like the wine at the marriage at Cana, the best comes last. Without my husband Charlie I could not even have begun this book, let alone finish it! Already an author himself he has tirelessly given me his wisdom and advice (constructive!) and ceaselessly answered my innumerable and often exasperating questions, always with patience, humour and affection. He has talked me down from my cliffs, inspired me with confidence, delivered me from a thousand IT crises, and somehow produced an inexhaustible supply of encouragement. Many husbands do noble things, but you surpass them all! Thank you Charlie. . .you have parented five children of destiny with me, and your partnership in this different creative work has equally been a delight. My gratitude is beyond measure.

PART 1

1

Unless a Seed Fall to the Ground

*Death be not proud, though some have called thee Mighty
and dreadful, for thou art not so.*

(John Donne)

Like a sharply focused photograph, I remember the room quite clearly. A crowd of well-dressed, smiling Americans were seated at round tables, enjoying a copious meal after an address from the Hispanic evangelist. I don't recall much of what he said, but I clearly remember his small, taut form and the energy that poured forth as he exhorted his listeners to pray for the souls in Silicon Valley and the Bay area, and earnestly lamented the decline of American society. I remember that he was dark and had a certain attractiveness and that he was accompanied by more than one very glamorous woman with big hair, nail polish on long nails, bright colours, well-fitting suits and heels. Newly arrived and rather bemused, I remember trying to add things up and thinking there was something amiss, though I couldn't quite identify it.

Of course we were pretty tired, partly from jet-lag, partly

from sheer excitement at having arrived for three months in the dream destination of California, but perhaps most of all because we had a new baby, only two-and-a-half months old, who had been restive since our arrival and had given us broken nights.

Now, as the meal drew to an end, the room was full of people milling around, and our host for the day, David, was introducing us to a steadily growing number of people. It was exciting to have been brought to this meeting, and very thoughtful of our hosts and dear friends, Celia and Stuart McAlpine, to have released us by baby-sitting for three children. Everything was new and fascinating in what I saw as a romantic wonderland, and the months stretched out ahead of us, full of promise and interesting meetings, events and trips. For a start the next day, January 24th, was my birthday and a champagne breakfast was planned. A champagne breakfast! Whoever heard of such an indulgence! Well, I was certainly up for it as a birthday treat.

We had come for an extended placement as part of my husband Charlie's training for ordination in the Church of England and had somehow persuaded ourselves and our theological college that close observation of a Pentecostal church, where our friend Stuart was Principal of the attached school, would be the best preparation for ministry in a British parish. More seriously it was an opportunity that presented itself to widen our vision and stretch our theological education. Added to this, it was a chance to spend time with close friends. Indeed, the goodness of God was boundless, and we were people with grateful hearts as we basked in this extraordinary treat that he had afforded us. Sometimes I could barely believe that we were on the road to becoming a pastoral couple; to fulfilling our dream of building a local church.

Suddenly, David, who had briefly left our sides, pushed his way unnaturally quickly through the crowded room and said, 'We've got to go. Now. I've had a call from Stuart and something's wrong with Samuel. Come on.'

'What's wrong?' I said, following him out of the room with Charlie. 'What's wrong?' I repeated, more loudly and with less control.

'I don't know,' replied David, 'Stuart didn't know.'

'What do you mean, he didn't know? How can you not know?'

And so the questions without answers succeeded each other until we were speeding along the motorway in silence, all three locked in our own thoughts, and David staring ahead, his jaw set. Road signs, directions, advertising billboards loomed up and were gone, almost lulling me like music as the clammy hand of fear tightened its grasp. As we passed a sign reading 'Hospital: 300 metres', my stomach lurched and the first tears spilt over the edge. I turned to Charlie silently pleading for help as my face crumpled, and he reached an arm round me, but I could see he was frightened too. Then, with David, he began to pray. Raising their voices, they began to call on God; that he would drive out whatever was threatening Samuel, that he would heal and restore; and running soon out of words, they lifted their voices in heavenly languages. I remained mute, my whole body paralysed with a fear that was now uncontrollable, feeling myself to be in a reality outside time, in which the sole element was pain that might last for ever. Only it wasn't real.

The car turned into our road and in the distance we saw

a figure standing outside the McAlpines' gate. As we drew closer we could see that it was Stuart, his face ashen, his body rigid. 'Drive to the hospital,' he ordered tersely.

'Stuart, what's happened, what's wrong, is he all right, will he be all right, how did it happen, he will be all right, won't he?' Our garbled questions matched the hope draining out of our bodies, our hearts, our minds.

'I don't know; I don't know,' repeated Stuart. 'He wasn't responding properly when I went to check him.'

San Jose, the capital of Silicon Valley, is a geometrically designed city, like so many in America. Left, right, right, left, right; we swung from street to street, almost rhythmically. There were no sweeping bends, none of the unpredictability of the English road system with its idiosyncratic and haphazard layout; just 90 degree turns, one upon another, and they seemed to go on for ever. I wondered if I would ever get there, if I would ever see Samuel again, ever hold him in my arms again. The city which this morning almost literally sparkled with light was this afternoon as grey and menacing as a mausoleum.

Turning yet another anonymous corner as David silently followed Stuart's clipped instructions, we came suddenly upon the huge, faceless institution, rising like a grey and gloomy giant out of nowhere. Suddenly Celia appeared, running towards us, her dark hair flying round her face. Getting out of the car, with a curious sense of slow motion and what felt like a Herculean effort, I fell into her arms.

'Ani,' she said, 'Samuel will be yours for all eternity.'

It was January 23rd, 1982.

The blow, when it came, hit me head on. Inside me the noise of its impact resounded as in an echo chamber. In an instant my life unravelled with the speed of lightning, and chaos replaced order. Focus gave way to blurred vision and the next moments—or was it hours?—seemed to take place in another dimension, at another remove, through a glass darkly; although my hearing was unimpaired, I just couldn't reach people. Most terrible of all I couldn't reach Samuel. It's curious what tiny details make their way into the memory files at a time like this. The doctor was tall, young and had fair hair and he said, very gently, 'The child is not alive.'

I heard, but I didn't believe. A nurse led us, with Stuart and Celia, into the innards of the great, grey hospital, and then to a room in the centre of which, on a full-sized hospital bed, lay the tiny, motionless body of our only son, Samuel, 'asked of God'. Of course he wasn't really dead, because he couldn't be. Every fibre of my being rose up to refuse the sight before me. He would soon revive, we would take him home, and the doctor would help us.

'Sudden Infant Death Syndrome,' the doctor was saying, 'is a relatively common phenomenon; there is no real explanation for it, although progress is being made through research.'

I still wasn't registering. For I knew he must be talking about someone else and that crib death, or cot death as it is known in the UK, had nothing to do with us. It was strange, though, I admitted to myself in a fleeting moment of lucidity, that he should be talking about this here in this room, and now.

With infinite tenderness, and beginning his own journey through the valley of the shadow of death, Charlie bent over the bed and took Samuel's lifeless, already bluish and stiffening frame in his arms, seeming to impart new life, willing him to come back. As if at a signal, though none was given, he and Stuart lifted their voices, just as he and David had done hours earlier, and commanded the spirit of death to let go, and the child to rise in the name of Jesus. Their prayers continued for several minutes, but Samuel didn't move. We stayed for some time, and I stared uncomprehendingly at my son, an unutterable grief expanding like a hot iron in my chest. Yet I made no move to hold him and, to this day, I don't know why. Perhaps I knew instinctively that he wasn't there any more, and that, much as I loved this child and fiercely longed for him to return, the inert body before me was just that: a body, a tent.

'Now,' says Paul, 'we know that if the earthly tent we live in is destroyed, we have a building from God, an eternal house in heaven, not built by human hands.'[1] And a little earlier, 'The body that is sown is perishable, it is raised imperishable; it is sown in dishonour, it is raised in glory; it is sown in weakness, it is raised in power; it is sown a natural body, it is raised a spiritual body.'[2]

We had to leave him, hard as it was. I think I probably knew, with a mother's instinct, that he was gone, long before we got to the hospital, but now we had to go, and no mother wants to leave her child unprotected, however irrational her desire.

Still in my world of chaos, I hammered on heaven's door. 'How could you let this happen? You promised him to me. . .'

Two months earlier, two thousand miles away from that hospital room so imbued with death, we were gathered excitedly in another hospital room, where two little girls had come to welcome their new brother. Two months earlier we were overwhelmed with joy, excitement and gratitude as we welcomed Samuel into the world, when the summer was ended and the winds of November were howling, snatching up the leaves and plucking at the coats that people pulled tightly around them. Now Samuel was dead. One hospital room is much like another; it is a place of work; of deliverance to life, or from sickness and death, if possible. But it is not always possible, and hospitals are houses of death for many. All that distinguishes one hospital room from another is what triumphs or tragedies of humankind are being played out in them.

All of us weeping, all of us in the surreal world that accompanies death, we drove slowly home. For the moment not even intelligible questions could be formed, and my mind was a scramble, the very worst sort of computer crash, the work of years irretrievably lost in an instant. Worse than that was the pain, hard to locate and intensifying by the minute, spreading slowly all over my body. Samuel, asked for and granted, was today lying stiff under a sheet in an anonymous morgue in a hospital. Not really, of course. Soon I would wake up and this terrible nightmare would fade away, like the times when I would wake to Charlie's voice gently speaking my name as I rose out of a confused scenario in which he was leaving me. Just as those increasingly infrequent dreams related back to Oxford days, so this event would simply reflect the earlier fear that I was not pregnant after all.

Soon a cup of tea was put into my hands and my little daughters were running into my arms and clambering onto my lap, elbowing one another out of the way. Stuart and Celia's two small children circled about us excitedly, and there seemed to be quite a lot of people and movement in the house, and they all seemed quite real; frighteningly real. Because if they were real and this was not after all a dream, it meant that Samuel was really dead, was really not going to breathe any more, and my arms, though now around my daughters, would not hold him to me again. All these thoughts brought unbearable pain, as did catching sight of Celia's rounded belly, home for the moment to their third child.

'Let's just gather together and honour the Lord and proclaim that God is God, even in the face of death.' The voice that spoke was deep and rich, had a strong Scottish accent and belonged to Gramps. Gramps and Mabs, or Campbell and Shelagh McAlpine, Stuart's parents, had moved to the States in the early 80s. They had embraced their children's friends with open arms and already been wise counsellors to us who were so new to the things of God.

Campbell would often appear unannounced at breakfast time, his arms laden with doughnuts, his face beaming, and stand beneficent as the four children hurled themselves at him shrieking with delight. In response to the patriarchal generosity represented by such simple acts, a spontaneous well of love had sprung up in my heart for him and Shelagh.

Now all of us were confronted with calamity, and we were suddenly in much more urgent need of parents. Somehow we were all collected together, including the children, in the spacious sitting room. Bread and wine had appeared on the table and the cacophony of our arrival gave way to a respectful quiet. What followed was one of the most significant moments in the whole process of living through the death of Samuel. Quietly, simply and with great authority, Stuart led us through a celebration of communion. We partook, in all our disarray, of the body and the blood, and, led by Stuart, we proclaimed that Christ is risen and that he lives today and that nothing can dim the power and the truth of this historical fact, not even a blow from the dark such as the one from which we were all reeling, even as he spoke.

'For I am convinced that neither death nor life, neither angels nor demons, neither the present nor the future, nor any powers, neither height nor depth, nor anything else in all creation, will be able to separate us from the love of God that is in Christ Jesus our Lord.'[3]

Somehow I got hold of this; somehow the powerful, all-embracing words of the Bible rang wonderfully true, crazed as I was with pain and desperately yearning to hold my son and feel his heartbeat. Somehow I was able to compute that, though 'things fall apart, the centre cannot hold,'[4] there was meaning and order to be retrieved, and that true reality lay not in the chaos of what had befallen us but in the eternal purposes of God.

Samuel's funeral took place a few days later. We chose to have him buried in San Jose, in the children's area of the huge city cemetery. Perhaps, had we had more time and less pain, we might have made other choices, but we have since made several visits to California, despite the enormous distance; and been able to sit around his grave with our daughters and the two children born to us later, and thank God for his goodness and for giving us a treasure in heaven.

Being able to return to California relatively often has been important for those two little daughters as they have

grown up. In the turmoil of events surrounding the immediate aftermath of Samuel's death, we made a decision not
to bring them to the funeral; a decision we have bitterly
regretted since, though it was no doubt made with the best
of intentions. It was our first real brush with death, and we
didn't understand the importance of saying goodbye, until
we did it ourselves that blustery January day.

Campbell presided over and preached at the funeral, and
it was a declaration of life over death. I, normally so timid
about such things, but curiously liberated by the enormity
of what was happening to me, lifted my voice and led the
congregation in a song. It didn't seem to matter so much
what people thought. 'I will enter his presence with thanks-
giving in my heart...' I sang. How could I have given utter-
ance to such words? Could it have been the courage and
consolation of the Holy Spirit?

The funeral parlour director had greeted us kindly and
with compassion on our arrival and led us in to see the tiny
coffin. 'He's all ready,' he said, 'Cute as a bug's ear.' To this
day, I've never understood that phrase, but I suppose it's a
florid way of saying tidy and tiny. After the service the
solemn cortege wound its way up to the children's section
where the cemetery workers had dug a fresh grave and
were waiting to fill it in. I remember a light drizzle falling
and the little box being awkwardly lowered. I remember
my long inward cry, echoing in the chamber of my spirit;
'Eloi, Eloi, lama sabachthani?'; 'My God, my God, why have
you forsaken me?'[5]

Now we had to live on.

2
Double Blessing

For some time after a death, every morning brings a painful rebirth into reality. Swimming into consciousness from powerfully realistic dreams in which Samuel was, for example, returned to us having been found lying swaddled in a graveyard, took a heavy toll on my emotional energy, already so decimated. I remember one morning being so convinced by my dream, so relieved and excited to see the pink cheeks and feel the warm breath against my breast, that it was hard for Charlie to break the truth to me again, and provoked an anguished bout of sobbing before the day had really begun.

When both members of a couple are in extreme pain and the need for relief more acute than any other impulse, all defence systems are on red alert and any concern for the welfare of the other is at its lowest ebb. We soon began to grow irritable with one another and, although we would weep in one another's arms at night, we each sensed the other's inability to really nurture the void of the loss with comforting words or to bring solace to our souls. Not surprisingly we became fractious and over-reacted to the slightest word or gesture that seemed less than gentle. When a wound is raw, the merest touch triggers a startled jerk away from the source of the touch, usually accompanied by a yelp of pain; and in this uncomfortable way we spent many of those early days on the journey of bereavement, hobbling through the valley of the shadow of death. Certainly we were a pitiful sight to the eyes of the God into whose hands we had confidently placed our lives and futures several years earlier.

Needless to say, this fragility affected our physical relationship. To me, nothing seemed more inappropriate—even vulgar and distasteful—than the idea of making love, and I shied away from anything that might have been construed as an amorous approach, turning away and drawing my knees up to my chest with a despairing moan. Didn't I realise his need of comfort? And didn't he realise my paralysis and the impossibility of arousal in the face of this monster? Didn't he realise the storm cloud of thoughts that broke with the merest suggestion of sex? Making love might lead to conception; conception to pregnancy; and all those changes and tiredness and a huge belly and the pain. . .and all, all for nothing, for Samuel was gone. Inside me, another wave of anguish would surge up.

Later, I would realise that Charlie's needs were equally authentic. Somehow we muddled through. Sex is an area of potential conflict during a time of bereavement and has shipwrecked many couples. It requires understanding and patience from both sides. At the time all we knew was that we were hurting one another with our unreasonable demands.

Apart from the Holy Spirit himself and the comforting

presence of Jesus, there were three things that saved us from the potential destructiveness latent in any such life-changing event. In fact, I believe that these three things are always the agents that God seeks to employ for help and healing. They are the natural family, friends and the body of Christ. In our case, having made the decision to stay in America, our own families could do little to help us, and I believe that in many ways it was a painful time for them as they felt our pain but could not hold and console us.

So it was with our friends, Stuart and Celia, and with the wider family of the church that we had come to America to observe, that we would initially experience some very deep healing. As things turned out, we were going to observe a lot more than we had expected of this church. We will look more closely at the subjects of family, friends and church in later chapters.

In the middle of one night, tossing and tormented, not wanting to wake Charlie from what little sleep he had and knowing he had no reserves for me, I crept into their bedroom and under the blankets next to Celia. My body was aching for Samuel and for human touch. How shocking! Or was it? There are a thousand images of those days, like a photograph album that captures a life, and this is one of the clearest, quite in focus, a pure and precious moment of balm.

Although they too were living through shock and grief, coming to terms with having found Samuel blue in his bed on that dreaded day, and knowing their own third child to be bursting with health in his mother's womb, their faith didn't waver for an instant.

'Even youths grow tired and weary,' says Isaiah, one of the Bible's prophets, 'and young men stumble and fall; but those who hope in the Lord will renew their strength. They will soar on wings like eagles; they will run and not grow weary, they will walk and not be faint.'[1] They soared, and ran and walked. They were a fountain of life to us, from that moment at the hospital until we waved a final and tearful goodbye as we boarded the plane to go home; and well beyond, of course; miles and seas are no obstacles to friendships forged like these.

The next morning, there was a knock at the door and Celia came into our room. 'Darlings,' she said, 'here's tea.' She gently put the tray down beside Charlie, came round the bed and sat down by me. 'Listen to this,' she said, 'Psalm 91.' She read it out and our eyes spilled over again. 'He who dwells in the shelter of the Most High will rest in the shadow of the Almighty. I will say of the Lord, "He is my refuge and my fortress, my God, in whom I trust."'[2]

What? No terror at night, no arrow by day; no pestilence from the dark, no destroying plague in broad daylight; no harm befalling us, no disaster coming near us? What could this possibly mean in the light of our present circumstances? All these things had, rather, combined their forces to strike us with one gigantic blow, and we lay slain beneath them. So why did I feel a curious warmth stealing into my tired and aching, exhausted limbs? I could not deny that, despite the seeming contradictions, my heart was strangely comforted by these words.

Later, I would understand that, no matter what happens, if we do make the Most High our refuge, he will be just that, and though we walk through the valley of the shadow of death, we will fear no evil, for he is with us and his rod and staff comfort us.

'Though he slay me, yet will I live,' says Job. Deep in the being of this blameless and upright man who has lost everything is a knowledge inscribed there by God, that defies his earthly circumstances by faith, and causes him to prophesy: 'I know that my Redeemer lives, and that in the end he will stand upon the earth. And after my skin has been destroyed, yet in my flesh I will see God.'[3]

Job, like Stephen and like Paul hundreds of years later and like John the Divine in the book of Revelation, was seeing heaven opened; and in a much lesser way (though a way that I believe to be available and accessible to all who cry out for it), as I huddled weakly in the refuge spoken of by the psalmist, I too gained a glimpse of heaven. I began to grasp that 'Christ has indeed been raised from the dead, the first-fruits of those who have fallen asleep.'[4] About eight years earlier in Cambridge I had assented to this intellectually: now I was faced with a chance to apply what I claimed to believe, and a decision made in safety needed to be ratified in danger. My faith certainly hung in the balance by moments. I do not write as one who has never wavered, nor doubted, but here the clouds parted to reveal a shaft of light; the sort that makes you take a sharp intake of breath as you walk by the sea under a setting sun, and something quickens your inmost being.

Celia had brought us this psalm with the quiet confidence of one who knows her Father in heaven. Through it I began too to understand that the perishable must clothe itself with the imperishable and the mortal with immortality; then the saying that is written will come true: 'Death has been swallowed up in victory.'[5] What did all this mean? Inevitably these early days were an emotional helter-skelter, and some of them were passed in an excess of weeping. But we talked and talked without stopping, questioning and railing at God, and these precious friends never once gave us the impression that they were bored or exhausted by our clinging needs; on the contrary, they lavished upon us their time, their imagination and their inexhaustible love.

They sent us out to the shopping mall to stroll around and buy clothes. A strange idea, you think perhaps? Yet this was the time when we understood the therapeutic value of shopping, even though our purchasing was minimal; it was the drifting with a disengaged mind that soothed us, though it brought us face to face with an early hurdle in bereavement.

Everyone, but everyone, had a tiny baby in a smart American stroller. How was it that the mall was filled exclusively with young couples shining with health and energy? Was this an area with a particularly high birth rate? Was it perhaps a mall reserved for young families?

Such are the slightly deranged thoughts of the grieving mind, and they are a normal part of the process of adapting to a new reality. One's whole being is straining toward the unattainable, and there is an intensity of focus, a sort of visual concentration that automatically sifts out uninteresting material.

Celia took me out to have my hair done and I had a frothy American perm. I remember the particular kindness of the woman who affected this rather dramatic transformation of my hair. Did she know?

The Saturday after Samuel died we all set off, with our four children, for a day out at Carmel. Carmel is a beautiful resort for the rich, with palm-lined avenues dividing gorgeous weatherboard properties. The shops are seductive and the restaurants irresistible, and at the time Clint Eastwood was the mayor, which rather added to the kudos; but we were there to walk the wide white shores for which the town is equally famed and, if truth be told, to pass some of this endless time which surprised us by continuing despite the death of our son. Contrasting with the natural beauty around us, the skies were leaden and a grey pall hung over the place. Acute pain had given way to a dull and heavy ache, and for all of us the day was desperately dreary, despite our best efforts to run with the children and exchange inconsequent remarks.

If Celia's gift was in a supernatural capacity to love and mother all at the same time, Stuart would draw us out with laughter. He has a wit second to none, and within days of Samuel's death we had broken a certain sound barrier, and felt our muscles uncoil as we all gave way to unrestrained mirth. At first we felt guilty: surely grieving must be a serious business and we should be circumspect in its presence? But we could sense the beneficial effect on our taut bodies. We talked about this together too and decided that laughing was doing us more good than harm, and that neither Samuel nor God would mind. On that day in Carmel, as the 'What if?' questions periodically and unpredictably made us wince, I remember a hilarious exchange between Stuart and a policeman who had halted our car, that made us all rock with laughter, then fall abruptly silent, wondering about the appropriateness of our reaction.

A month or so later, they sent us away for a weekend alone together, again at Carmel. We set off in a borrowed car, feeling at once elated and agonised. It was good for them and it was good for us. Here, in a little hotel we made fragile steps towards recovering our intimacy; we were reassured by our love for one another, shaken as we were by the recent hurricane. We went to see the film *Chariots of Fire* and became intoxicated with the soaring music and the glory of Eric Liddell's integrity. To this day, the music of Vangelis is bound up for us with Samuel and it echoed in our minds as we walked the dunes and gazed out to sea, each absorbed in the business of trying to reconcile the undeniable majesty of God with the unacceptable loss of our son.

March came, and with it the appointed day for our return to the UK. New mountains rose up before us out of the mist, and we clung to Stuart and Celia as we parted amid many tears and prayers in the impersonal atmosphere of the airport.

Many loving arms reached out for us as we returned to Bristol to pick up the threads of an English life that we had left so differently, so full of confidence and joy. The first hurdle, we knew, was to unlock our front door and climb the stairs to Samuel's bedroom, arrayed like a museum caught in time with his clothes, his toys, the pictures on the wall. Here was a welcome for someone who would never come. Here was a cupboard that needed clearing out when we had the strength. Dear little Hannah and Alice, by now accustomed to their parents' weeping, patiently accompanied them in this painful rediscovery of a home.

Among my papers and documents was my Child Benefit book. One day, feeling stronger, I walked up the road to the Post Office to hand it in. Waves of defeat washed over me and each step became harder to take. 'How are you? We've had a wonderful time in America.' (Had we?) 'But a terrible thing happened.' I struggled to control my voice. I explained falteringly. The official, sympathetic voice reached my ears through the perspex pane separating customer from state. My raw and heightened emotions detected the distant volcanic rumble in my troubled soul that heralded another bout of weeping as this relatively small but sharp consequence of death sliced into my delicate world with the precision and power of a butcher's knife. My stomach contracted as the familiar sinking feeling spread effortlessly through my body with the ease of a cloud obscuring the sunlight. My eyes prickled. I pushed the crumpled book under the glass, and turned, focusing on the door, through which I passed as the wave broke. Retracing my steps home, I railed at God: 'Why did you do this? Why did you take him away? Why didn't you protect him? Why? Why? Why? How could you? Are you God?'

In December 1981, three weeks after Samuel's birth, we had made a visit to a parish in Essex, with Samuel, where Charlie had been offered a job as a curate. Although anywhere within striking distance of the Dartford Tunnel would normally have been excluded from consideration, we had decided to pursue this avenue, albeit with some uncertainty, as a good friend whom we had met and made during the years at Trinity theological college in Bristol had contacted us and energetically persuaded us to do so. He had moved to the same parish a year earlier and was excited by the potential of this London overspill community, with its population of upwardly mobile and positive people. The thought of being able to work with friends mollified our prejudiced dislike of the geography.

Seven months later we sold our house in Bristol, packed up and drove back to Essex with our two little girls and Samuel's painful and tangible absence. The Bristol chapter was ended, a page had turned and the blank pages of our first job in the Church of England lay before us; a bleak and un-inviting landscape on that day. But time was performing its silent stealthy work of healing, not least in the intimacy of our marriage. As summer ended and the leaves turned again, I found I was pregnant for the fourth time, and together we found joy again in the midst of a strange concoction of conflicting emotions. An emotional rollercoaster ensued, as powerful memories of carrying Samuel blended with surges of hope and daring excitement about this new child.

'New house, new baby!' smiled the kindly people of our new parish, where the days began to pass by more quickly again, full of introductions, new routines and the milestone of primary school for Hannah. In November we celebrated Samuel's first birthday with a special tea for the girls. We put one candle on the cake and pored over all the photos we had of him. This was not a morbid occasion; far from it. The sit-ting room was festooned with cards from family and friends and from many members of our new church, who had tire-lessly and selflessly laboured to make us feel welcomed and loved. They had embraced us in our loss and entered some-how into our suffering with us, thus drawing in some meas-ure the sting of death. In the cosy warmth of our sitting room, the curtains drawn against the dark November evening and the wind whisking leaves along our suburban street, a small miracle took place. We found our hearts filling with grat-itude and strangely warmed. Hope was stealing back and we spoke out our thanks to God, whom we had raged at so often since that black day in January, in a simple family prayer time. As Hannah and Alice uttered their sweet little thank yous, an overpowering affection for them rose up inside me like a dam bursting, and I silently acknowledged the healer. It was a turning point on the road to wholeness.

The next hurdle was Christmas without Samuel, two stockings instead of three, but midwinter had passed by then and my belly was swelling with the new life that spoke to us all of a future and of hope. Days turned to weeks, weeks to months, and the days grew longer as the world turned towards another spring. Early one Sunday morning in April, the onset of contractions warned us of the imminent arrival of the baby, and we set off for the hospital. My thoughts and emotions were not surprisingly in chaos and turmoil. I was excited, but I was afraid. Hannah had been born by caesarean, Alice and Samuel with the help of forceps: all three births had been lengthy and painful. Would this be too? I felt faint at the prospect of all the pain: 'O Lord, please help me.'

The labour intensified, and my undivided concentration was needed for the huge upheaval that giving birth brings to the body. There was no mental space to think about Samuel or to be fearful for this new child; nor did I ponder on the sex of the infant so nearly with us. As the pain increased, so somehow did my ability to bear it, and to my incredulity my prayer seemed to be answered as the instruction to push came much sooner than during the previous births. After what then did seem a long time, I heard the words I hadn't dared to hope I would ever hear again:

'It's a boy!'

The words came swimming through the haze of exhaustion and the whirl of delivery room activity, and as if from somewhere far, far away. For a fleeting second, other words pronounced in another hospital, superimposed themselves, fading to the echo. . .It's a boy! It's a boy!

'Is it? Are you sure? Is it? Is it really? Oh, Charlie. . .' A dreamlike euphoria engulfed me, an intensity of joy and amazement that comes but infrequently in a lifetime. It was about four hours since we had arrived and I had given birth without forceps. A tiny boy lay on my breast. And I lay on the hospital bed, laughing and crying, my eyes meeting Charlie's in our unspoken ecstasy. John Samuel, to be known as Jack, had arrived.

The congregation, voices lifted in worship, fell silent as their young curate strode up the aisle with a broad smile on his face. They held their breath as one, waiting for the news. . .what would it be?

'It's a boy,' said Charlie, but he could say no more, for the people erupted with clapping, cheering and weeping with joy. This was the church as God intended, and this was a day of destiny.

It was to be many years before I understood this, for I had yet to become aware of my own destiny and conscious that I had been made in the secret place, woven together in the depths of the earth. It had not been revealed to me that all my days had been written in God's book of life before one of them came to be. It is important to underline that every child, humanly wanted or unwanted, planned or un-planned, is known and called by God. Every child has a potentially assured future and his paths mapped out by heaven. But creation itself is groaning because it is in the grip of decay and destruction and many of the perfect plans of the Lord are aborted. Jack would be almost 20 by the time the mists cleared and I felt I received a little understanding about the destiny of each next generation.

PART 2

3

Made to Measure

What is destiny?

There's a divinity that shapes our ends,
Rough-hew them how we will.
(William Shakespeare)

On November 2nd, 2003, the service was drawing to a close at St Aldate's Church in Oxford. Twenty years had passed since that day in April 1983. We had spent ten of them in Essex and the other ten in Paris, returning to England in 2002 for Charlie to take up the appointment of our dreams as he became Rector of this student church for all nations.

The preacher was Ugandan John Mulinde, a man who had become a close friend since we met him in 1997 in Paris. The day before, the church had been full of people attentively listening to John addressing the question and title of our weekend conference: 'Can a nation be changed?' He had talked of being set apart for God and what that means; of the power of Western world systems to control us; of holiness; of desperate prayer. This evening he was tired, not surprisingly, and finding it difficult to engage what by any standards can be a daunting audience. We conferred quietly and a little anxiously on the front row about how to facilitate a response to what he was saying. Closing his Bible, John bowed his head and invited the congregation to stand.

Suddenly, I knew what to say and, going to the microphone, I began to speak. 'Lots of you are tired of being lukewarm. You long to be all that God intends you to be, but are held back by the pace of life, the ease with which you can and frequently do postpone your pursuit of God. Make this a covenant with him, as your spirit has been stirred hearing what you know to be an authentic message coming from a life that matches the words.' Equally suddenly there was a rush of movement and people began to stream to the front of the church, many of them running and many of them young. Many fell to their knees, and tears began to flow. Some of us moved among them to offer prayer or simply bless the obvious engagement with God that was taking place. Where there had been dignified order five minutes earlier, there was now a noisy chaos with a hubbub of voices lifted to God. Half an hour later, as people were making their way home and the church was emptying, two young girls remained prostrate in front of the stage. Someone asked me whether I thought they were all right. 'They're all right!' I said, smiling. When I finally went to talk to one of them, she could barely speak and nodded her head in a drunken way in answer to my questions.

What was happening? Something that is not at all unique to one church in an English city, but common to churches in every denomination and in many nations. We are living in the days of an unprecedented awakening around the world and God is calling the next generation in unprecedented numbers. Nation after nation is experiencing outbreaks of young people not only turning to God, but doing so in a radical way. That is to say, they are not interested in the form of religion, but in the power of the cross to save and deliver, and they are unafraid. They know they were born for something and instinctively they know that to discover that something they have to discover God.

I think of large youth movements, such as Soul Survivor, Timothy Camp, or Passion, gathering multitudes of teens and young adults hungry for God, and for whom Sunday is not enough. Words are not enough either, and in the summer of 2002, Mission to Manchester saw thousands of youngsters descending on the city to paint houses, weed gardens, clear rubbish, run summer camps for schoolchildren, go shopping for the elderly and infirm, talk with the homeless and the drug addicts, and invite anyone they could to the huge celebrations held every evening. It was a massive operation that took a year to plan, had the support and co-operation of the Manchester Constabulary, and cost thousands. But they were undaunted by the size of the vision because it was a vision from God, and this is a generation with a passion to see communities transformed and the church overflow her walls. A similar project took place in July 2004 in London.

I think of The Call, a gathering of 600,000 young people in the Washington DC Mall in 2000 to spend the day pleading with God for their nation. No big names, no personalities to attract people: the publicity focused on the reason for the event. One after another, young boys and girls spoke passionately of their yearning that America return to God, a nation whose constitution declares, 'In God we Trust'. One of these was Michelle, now 21 years old and studying at Wycliffe Hall in Oxford, having spent a year as an intern with us at St Aldate's. She originally came to Oxford for just one term!

Crowd events come and go. Nonetheless they achieve things that we cannot measure, because someone has taken seriously a demand or requirement of God. In some small way the outworking of history and of individual lives is different because of the obedience of this someone. You cannot have a crowd without individuals. Let's look at some of the faces in the crowd.

I think of a young man who left Oxford shortly after our arrival to serve with a mission distributing medical supplies on the border of Congo and northern Uganda. War was raging between the two nations and it drew close to the compound where he lived and worked as an administrator. Gun battles were an almost daily occurrence outside the gate and men were slaughtered with machetes within yards of the mission.

I think of another young man who gave up a life of potential comfort to serve in Burundi, also an area of conflict, tribal in this case. Only in one sense he has given nothing up, for he held fast to nothing; it is his joy to follow Jesus where he calls. He writes of his feelings following a severe accident that befell a cousin in the UK, causing him to fly home from Burundi to visit her:

There are so many gifts that we take for granted and presume are rights. I want to shake the millions of people who are sacrificing everything to attain a certain standard of living, at the expense of having a life. I want to reach out to the millions who cram their lives and schedules so full while they themselves remain so empty. I want to give blood which can bring life to someone else. Debs has had literally dozens of units of blood pumped into her—three times what is in her body, but she has kept on losing most of it. It makes me think of the ultimate sacrifice of the One who gave his blood for me—what incredible love! And in turn I want to lay down my life in His service, be it Burundi or here.[1]

I think of Eric Liddell, the Scottish missionary who was also, and more famously, an Olympic athlete who gained a gold at the 1924 Games when he set a new world record for the 400 yards. Born in 1902 to missionary parents in Tientsin, northern China, Liddell's true notoriety sprang from his remarkable boldness in honouring God. He had qualified for the Olympics in the 100 yards, but on discovering that the heats were to be held on a Sunday, declined to participate and instead preached in a Parisian church. He agreed to run in the 400 yards, however, and despite not having trained for it won the race four metres ahead of the next runner. This event was brilliantly captured in the 1991 film, *Chariots of Fire*, in which Liddell says, 'God made me fast, and when I run, I feel his pleasure.' This is a pleasing expression of destiny, and not only pleasing but inspiring; David Puttnam, the producer of the film, is but one man who was affected: 'In many ways Liddell was the kind of person who, in my heart of hearts, I'd always dreamed of being. . .few lives have more to teach us about the virtues of honour and probity.'

Liddell returned to China to become a missionary in

1932, for all of his life was a race for the kingdom of God. There, growing political tensions caused him to send his pregnant wife and two daughters home, but Eric remained. He was interned in a Japanese camp in China in 1943 and died two years later of a tumour and typhoid.

The Cambridge genius mathematician and classicist Henry Martyn, who is pictured in the stained glass window at the east end of St Aldate's, forsook a distinguished career to become a missionary. He was moved by reading the journals of the puritan David Brainerd and stirred by hearing the great Charles Simeon recount stories of William Carey, the shoe cobbler who established a strong gospel witness in Bengal between 1792 and 1802. Despite opposition, Martyn was determined and, on arriving in Calcutta in 1806, he wrote in his journal, 'I almost think that to be prevented going among the heathen as a missionary would break my heart. . .I feel pressed in spirit to do something for God. . . I have hitherto lived to little purpose, more like a clod than a servant of God—now let me burn out for God.'

And this he did, dying at the age of 31, but not before he had employed his intellect to translate the New Testament into Persian, Arabic and Hindu, thus opening the way for thousands upon thousands to encounter the gospel.

I think too of the houses of prayer that are springing up across the nations. Church as we know it, gathering together for a few hours each week to celebrate our faith, is good, but no longer satisfying the increasingly desperate hunger for God rising around the world and in a particularly striking way in the next generation. Mike Bickle, of the International House of Prayer in Kansas City, describes his hunger:

As I knelt to pray in my office, little did I expect to receive a new direction that would result in experiencing an entirely new dimension of spiritual desire. I began to pray because an unusual quiet yearning had filled my heart. It grew as my heart was stirred, and it became an intense longing, a thirst that felt impossible to quench. 'Lord, seal me. Put the fiery love in me.' As the words of desire began to pour from my lips, the desire for God felt stronger and stronger, until it almost hurt. I began weeping, not from pain but from desire. But the longing for Christ only became more intense. . .Before long the room was filled with his wonderful, divine presence, and my heart was spilling over.[2]

American pastor Lou Engle explains the birth of constant prayer in his church:

Several years ago the Lord had been speaking to me concerning presenting before the Lord an offering of day and night worship and intercession. God had been calling me to a sense of longing for day and night intercession in Mott Auditorium, the building where our church gathers.

One day, up in my office, I was reading the testimony of Jim Goll who had taken an intercessory team to where the original Moravians were and where a 100-day prayer meeting of day and night intercession took place that launched a massive wave of missions. He said in this article that God was going to launch 120 of these houses of prayer in cities, and as I read that it just broke forth in my spirit and I began to weep and groan, 'Here, Lord, here. Mott Auditorium, 24-hour house of prayer.'

As I was groaning and weeping under the presence of the Lord, the phone rang, and there on the phone was a friend of mine. As I was weeping on the phone, I said, 'I'm just right now reading an article by this man named Jim Goll and this 24-hour house of prayer.'

He said, 'Lou, that's why I'm calling you right now. This very moment I was in a meeting and Jim Goll was preaching, and he just stopped in the middle of his message and said, 'Lou Engle, Mott Auditorium, 24-hour house of prayer.' I was blown away. I knew God was shouting to me.

Two years later, we went on a 40-day fast, we built a room only for prayer and we launched the vision of a 24-hour house of prayer. That morning I went to pray and the Lord began to put this prayer in my heart: 'Raise up a Moravian lampstand, raise up a Moravian lampstand.'

The Lord spoke to my heart Matthew 5:15: 'Neither do people light a lamp and put it under a bowl. Instead they put it on its stand, and it gives light to everyone in the house.'

And I felt like the Lord was saying, 'I am going to raise up this lampstand. The 24-hour house of prayer is going to give light. It is going to be brought out of its hiddenness and I am going to put it on its stand in the nations of the earth. Day and night, intercession will arise all over the globe. . .'[3]

Breaking off abruptly in the middle of a message, as Jim Goll is recorded doing in this story, seems a curious thing to do. But there are many instances of those who are prophetically gifted behaving in this way. I clearly recall listening to Joy Dawson, a noted teacher on intercession, at a conference and being amazed and alarmed as she suddenly stopped speaking, knelt down on the platform and left us all hanging in an uncomfortable silence for several minutes, before explaining that she had needed to listen to the Lord there and then. It seems that such people are in dialogue with God even as they teach or preach and subject to such interruptions.

I think of the prayer mountain a few miles outside Kampala; 'Africa Prayer Mountain for all nations', proclaims a large billboard as you crest the hill leaving the Entebbe road and the glimmering shores of Lake Victoria far below. Here you walk into an open heaven. You may not see, as another prophet, Isaiah, did, the Lord seated on a throne, high and exalted, but you will know that he is there and you will feel an almost tangible sense of his presence. Day in and day out, the 100 acres of the hill are inhabited by men and women, young and old, walking, weeping, pleading, prostrate as they pray, often with loud shouts and groaning for the nations of the world. Everywhere there are tents where those who come for extended periods of prayer and fasting spend the few hours necessary for sleep.

I think of the 24/7 prayer movement that has generated continuous prayer since 1999. Do I hear you say you can't compute that sentence? In the foreword to *Red Moon Rising*,[4] the account of how it all started, Floyd McClung explains:

In 1722 a rag-tag band of several hundred young people gathered on the estate of a wealthy count by the name of Zinzendorf. Five years later, God showed up and they began to pray. They prayed in strange and creative ways, but they prayed. They prayed 24/7. Their prayer led to compassion for the poor and those who had never heard of Jesus. Their prayer meeting went on for 125 years without ceasing—the longest prayer meeting in history.

God has decided to do again what he did among the Moravians almost 300 years ago. A 24/7 prayer meeting has started again, but now it has circled the globe overnight. We should not be surprised God chose an unlikely candidate to lead the 24/7 prayer movement. Pete Greig struggled to hear God's voice and wasn't very good at praying, but he was determined to chase the Spirit wherever that took him. . .he reminds us that prayer doesn't belong to the stodgy or the religious. Nor can prayer be controlled by religious types who think they have a corner on the right words to use, and the correct way to stand. 'Red Moon Rising'. . .stirs faith in us to believe that when we talk to God he responds.[5]

Pete Greig describes the impact of visiting Herrnhut, the village established by the ragtag band: 'We moved a mile or so down the road. . .to Berthelsdorf. Here. . .the community had gathered on 13th August 1727. As they committed themselves to unity, the Holy Spirit had moved so powerfully that some of the congregation, it is said, staggered from the building hardly able to stand.' For the Moravians, this moment was, 'the culmination of a process of renewal (three months earlier they had drawn up a "covenant for Christian living", something like a monastic rule of life). . . I knelt in a pew and said a little prayer, deeply conscious of the fact that an event in this building, almost exactly 272 years earlier was somehow still impacting my life at the dawn of the third millennium.' It was a life changing day. 'In many ways I left the apartment that morning as a tourist and returned as a pilgrim.'[6]

As such stories show, what we are seeing today is not a new phenomenon. Every historical revival has been preceded by intense and sustained prayer, from the eighteenth century revival in America spearheaded by Jonathan Edwards to the Hebridean revival in the mid-twentieth century. What many think to be new is the scale of what is happening. This is in part due to the capacity and speed of communication and the possibilities of disseminating information that have been opened up by technology for global man. At the same time there is a cry in the heart of this man for he knows that sophistication and intellect do not necessarily lead to altruism and philanthropy, nor up to the throne room of God. Rather they lead him up the blind alley of calling himself God. He knows that war, civil and international, slavery, hunger, sickness and murder ravage the face of the earth not less but more than in all the centuries of his history, and that we are no nearer our goal of peace on earth than we have ever been.

The next generation, children of the internet, global travellers who have more in common with the culture of their generation than their nation, are profoundly aware of the evil that is polluting the face of the globe like thick, suffocating smoke, exactly the image that was used by John Mulinde in a prophetic word that he offered when he first began to come to Europe during the 1990s:

> I saw the map of the continent of Europe and as I looked there came out of this map a big pillar of smoke. It was a tall thick and dark pillar of heavy black fumes as from a factory chimney. The fumes rose up very slowly and gradually began spreading out.
>
> From the pillar came a thin mist, and it began spreading out almost imperceptibly, but within a short time it had formed a dark film over the entire continent. As the mist grew thicker, the features below it blurred and became difficult to distinguish under the black fumes.[7]

Few would venture to disagree that this is a pertinent image for the Europe of today. The war that is greater in scope and goal and savagery than any currently scarring nations is the war between good and evil, between the Creator and his opponent, the one who fell like lightning from heaven and who has sought from that moment to seduce mankind from the safety of relationship with his Maker. This is the war towards the resolution of which history is slowly making its way. This is the war for which God is training up a generation of soldiers the like of which has never been seen in its breadth and determination. God's call and appointing is out for thousands of young men and women, and many of them know it. That is why they cannot abide hypocrisy in any shape or form; it's why they can smell the stench of dishonesty and double standards a mile off; it's why they are impatient when they find authenticity or integrity lacking; it's why they couldn't care less about style or form, but care passionately about content. They have long relinquished the desire to impress with appearance or money, to manipulate or to seek the power of control. They understand much better than many of their parents the true state of corruption in the nations. They understand too that neither politics nor humanism is going to unlock the door to peace in the nations.

War means casualties, and where a war between tribes or nations is concerned we understand this without any difficulty. We are beginning too to understand the concept of war as expressed through terrorism as we hear almost every day of another suicide bomber snatching away in an instant a handful or dozens or even hundreds of lives. Soldiers are dying each day while politicians seek to justify the need, and we briefly study their faces as they appear in our newspapers, wondering about the years, the experiences, the joys and sorrows looking out at us through their eyes.

We understand much less the notion of casualties in the other, bigger, universal war; the spiritual war. We do not make connections easily. In our day hundreds of lives are being snatched away, snuffed out or incapacitated, and we are not noticing. And if we do notice and lament, we do not understand that there is a master plan behind the loss. When God raised up Moses as a deliverer for the captive people of Israel, all hell broke loose in the form of an edict from the king of Egypt instructing the Hebrew midwives to kill baby boys on delivery. When the Magi ingenuously enquired of Herod, 'Where is the one who has been born King of the Jews?'[8] they did not realise that their question would lead to Herod signing the death warrant of scores of baby boys from newborns to two-year-olds. So during the absence of the infant Jesus in Egypt, the bitter sound of mothers wailing for their children resounded in the town and surroundings of Bethlehem. The plans and purposes of God were not thwarted, cannot be thwarted, but there were casualties, there was loss of the most painful kind.

This is how I understand our personal loss of our firstborn son. Before he was born, in a time of great anxiety over my pregnancy, I asked for prayer at a church service, and the person who prayed did so in a prophetic way, implying that the child I was carrying was marked out by God for a future. At the same time a GP had diagnosed an abnormal pregnancy and advised a D&C. So it would be possible to think that his life was already contested at this stage. Not, of course, by the GP, who was simply doing his job as best he could, but by forces of another order. Only the wisdom of an elderly doctor prevented Samuel's death even earlier than it happened. This is the story of one person, and it is surely repeated in literally millions of lives, each made unique by its details.

Today we have passed laws, beginning in 1967, to legalise the killing of millions of unborn infants. And we have done it in the name of human rights. I, a potential mother, have so much legal control over my own body that I may choose to end the life of a child I have conceived by the freedom to have intercourse. Clearly the most obvious caveat to this is in the case of a rape. While rape is one of the worst travesties of human relations, any infant that may be procreated in the process is not to blame, and so clearly punishment by death should not be his lot. Heather Gemmen's powerful testimony in her book, *Startling Beauty*, where she tells of her lovely daughter conceived in a terrifying and traumatic rape reminds us how little we can see of our children's future and how vital it is that we do right by them however they are conceived. Thousands of children are conceived in far from ideal circumstances, yet their lives are not taken from them. Where do we draw the line? I know two people who were conceived through rape, and neither of them wishes, as Job does at one point, that they had never seen the light of day, although both, like him, have suffered severe trials and the pain of loneliness. Job, to whom a whole book of 42 chapters in the Bible is devoted, was just an upright man who respected God and resisted evil. Many tragedies befall him, yet he steadfastly refuses to blame God, even when his wife exhorts him to do so.

The next generation is not being picked off by abortion

alone. They are selling their souls for drugs, for sex, for alcohol, for a multitude of bondages. We have told them that God is dead, but they know they need him. Douglas Coupland confesses this need at the close of his book, *Life After God*:

> Now here is my secret. . .I tell it to you with an openness of heart that I doubt I shall ever achieve again, so I pray that you are in a quiet room as you hear these words. My secret is that I need God—that I am sick and can no longer make it alone. I need God to help me give, because I no longer seem to be capable of giving; to help me be kind, as I no longer seem capable of kindness; to help me love, as I seem beyond being able to love.[9]

What a cry! Who will answer? There is a calling on this next generation, a calling to recognise and embrace their destiny, and their destiny is to be unashamed followers of Jesus and to call their own and other generations back to him. It is to proclaim his word and remove the shame of the church and the mockery of the nations, and to become a new breed of reformers who will seek to eradicate world poverty and hunger and call the nations to respect the planet (which we were commanded to care for long before the creation of church or missions) through their engagement with ecological issues. It is to unlock heaven through their prayers and release the revival of God-focused worship throughout the earth; in other words to be the agents of ushering millions into the kingdom of God. I believe God has been speaking through his prophets about this.

Prophets are often strange people, none more so perhaps than some of those who straddle the pages of the Old

Testament. I have often wondered what the church would make of Ezekiel, who spoke of fantastical visions,[10] and who was apparently instructed by God to prophesy the coming siege of Jerusalem by making a model of the city, placing an iron pan between the model and himself to symbolise a wall, then lying down first on one side, then the other, tied with ropes to symbolise immobility until the days allotted to the visual aid are completed. All this to warn of the following: 'Son of man, I will cut off the supply of food in Jerusalem. The people will eat rationed food in anxiety and drink rationed water in despair, for food and water will be scarce. They will be appalled at the sight of each other and will waste away because of their sin.' Certainly such an event would make it to the pages of our national newspapers, for we love the quirky and the bizarre, as evidenced by the speed with which we highlight anything that is strange, such as the long-forgotten individual who once suspended himself in a perspex cube over the Thames for days on end.

Prophets are strange and their prophecies need to be considered carefully, as discernment and wisdom are sought for their interpretation. This is the meaning of weighing a prophecy. Today our prophets are no less strange, but they are no less tuned into the voice of God either. One prophecy given about the call to this generation speaks of a great army of the Lord being raised up, who will be unafraid of living for Christ. It speaks of it being easier to die for Christ than to live for him, but that where a life is extinguished in the battle, ten more will rise to replace him or her. I first heard this word on tape while in the car. It was a bright autumn day and the rolling sunlit countryside of Oxfordshire provoked an outpouring of thanks to God for his kindness in bringing us home after our ten years in Paris. Straining to catch the words, I rewound repeatedly to make sure I was hearing correctly. The speaker was saying that he had 'heard' these things in October 1981. A month before Samuel's birth. This, he was saying, was a generation that would form a mighty army for the Lord. Just the mention of a date so special to me was, understandably, enough to trigger deep-seated emotion. I felt the presence of God close in the car, and a sudden burst of grief poured out in my tears. Perhaps only a small part of this word was wholly acceptable. Prophecy of the fore-telling rather than the forth-telling kind is always at the very most good in parts, like the proverbial curate's egg, and at the very least controversial. I am certainly not suggesting that it had any kind of author-ity; I am simply saying that such a word can bring encour-agement even to one person; what it did for me was to reignite my desire and energy to pray for my children and their generation. The function of prophecy, the New Testament tells us, is to instruct, encourage and edify.

If, like me, you are a parent to the next generation, God is calling you to recognise what is happening as God is un-deniably revealed to them, and to facilitate their response to him. This means accepting that sometimes they are wiser than us, they can see further, their fingers are more accu-rately on the spiritual pulse of the church, even of the nation. It means acknowledging that truths that have taken us years to appropriate have been grasped with alacrity and spiritual acumen by our children.

If you are somewhere between the ages of 15 and 32, two generations increasingly referred to as Millennials and Xers respectively, God is calling you too, and looking for an answer. He calls you not to give up the quest to discover who you were made to be and what you were made to do. No one would contest that this is a fearsome challenge in a postmodern age increasingly hostile to Christianity. God is surely calling you, and us your parents, to stand up and be counted, and to lobby and fight for righteousness.

So what is destiny?

It is not a question that can be answered definitively, of course, but there is no question that the passion we see in this generation and the rising tide of prayer pouring out of them are connected with destiny. The Bible says that the concept of eternity is written in the heart of man;[11] or to put it another way part of his DNA. Even those who reject God acknowledge this. Jean-Paul Sartre, the French existentialist philosopher, said; 'I don't see myself as so much dust that appeared in the world, but as a being that was expected, prefigured and called forth.' On another occasion he said, 'I caught the Holy Spirit in the basement of my life and flung him out.' That we have a destiny is inescapable; whether we find it and live it out, be it for two decades or ten, is a different matter entirely.

Supremely in all history, the person and life of Jesus speak of destiny. 'When the fullness of time came, God sent forth his Son. . .born under the law, to rescue those born under the law that we might receive adoption as sons.'[12]

The Christmas story is more than a story. It is God speaking into and shaping history to fashion the salvation of mankind: the perfect rescue for the dearest of all his creation who had spurned his love and cherished pride in their heart. Seven hundred years earlier the prophets had spoken of this. They told of his birth from a virgin, of where he would be born, of how he would die, and that he would be raised from the dead. Creation spoke of it, as a bright star led the wise men to the stable. And the world-wide Roman census that Caesar Augustus had decreed gave the backdrop to the Bethlehem stable stage. Jesus resisted every pressure to deviate him from his destiny. . .whether pressure from crowds to meet their needs, or to make him king, from Peter wanting to keep him safe,[13] or from his own fears as he prayed and sweated in the garden of Gethsemane.[14]

The exquisite story of Jesus Christ quintessentially captures the notion of destiny. . .and you must capture yours.

4

The Hearts of the Fathers

The destiny of reconciled generations

I held the sobbing girl gently, feeling the anguish she was expressing. Her eyes were red from rubbing them but being unable to stop the flow of tears. However, looking good, which she always did, being a very pretty girl, didn't matter right now. Several moments later she was just about ready to explain what was wrong..

'It's my father. He's so distant with me. He never seems to listen to me. He brushes me off. And I love him so much. . .' More tears.

We are living in an era of pronounced alienation between the generations. Mike Bickle, in his book, *The Pleasures of Loving God*, writes about Simeon and Anna, from the presentation of Jesus in the Temple found in Luke's gospel.

Simeon and Anna are wonderful testimonies of the significant things that can happen when senior saints in the body of Christ enter into the ministry of prayer and fasting. I believe that this type of ministry will occur again among young people, but there will always be a strong, dynamic contingent of elders who are praying and fasting across the world. The young people will be bonded to them as to mothers and fathers in the spirit. Adolescents will look into the eyes of their elders in the Lord and will wonder why they feel such a strong spiritual connection between them. Young people will look up to you, senior citizen, and say 'I don't know why, but I really like you.' You may smile knowingly because you were the one who birthed these young people into the kingdom of God.

Bickle's words express well that praying for the next generation does not concern only families related by blood. What about the unmarried? Where do they fit into the picture? What about those who are not able to have natural children? I believe that the call to become mothers and fathers is flung very wide by God. He is far more interested in our adulthood than in our particular circumstances, as far as the destiny of the next generation is concerned. He needs every soldier who will sign up.

I know myself the truth of what Bickle says. There are elderly saints in the family of God who elicit a response from the depth of my being that can often cause tears to flow. One such is Campbell McAlpine, one of the fathers of renewal during the 1960s. Of course he became very personally a father at the time of Samuel's death, which perhaps accounts partly for the strength of feeling. Another is John Wimber, but in his case I never knew him in more than a very superficial way, meeting him at conferences from time to time, and occasionally having the opportunity to pick his brains, such as when he visited us in Paris in 1995. Nonetheless I found a strength of feeling towards him that I can only account for as the bonding of the Spirit described by Bickle.

No man is able to be a father as God is a father, for every successive generation fathers out of its own pain and inadequacy. We should be careful not to apportion blame to our own fathers for the pain in the pit of our stomachs, for they too had their pain to carry.

Many experienced a strong attachment to Wimber, but curiously his relationship with his own father was tragically lacking. 'John grew up knowing almost nothing about the Wimbers. What he did know about his father didn't cause him to want to know any more.'[1] This only further confirms the notion that spiritual parenting can go well beyond natural.

Many fathers have an inexpressible longing to be a father in the mould of the heavenly Father, but are crippled by their own experiences as a son. Fathers can be withdrawn, emotionally repressed, drunken, violent or absent, among other things. So to know the Father's love is a foundational need for every human being, and it is God's desire that we should know it. To be a father in the Lord is a calling for every man who knows Christ. Paul, who was not a father of flesh, was an eminent example of a father of the Spirit, referring to Titus, 'my true son in our common faith',[2] to Timothy 'my dear son',[3] and to the Galatians as 'my dear children, for whom I am again in the pains of childbirth until Christ is formed in you'.[4] And though he predominantly addresses the Corinthians as brothers, he reverts to the parent image at moments of passion as opposed to persuasion. 'We have spoken freely to you, Corinthians, and opened wide our hearts to you. . .As a fair exchange—I speak as to my children—open wide your hearts also.'[5]

The same call pertains to being a mother. Again, my life

has been shaped to a certain extent by women who have modelled godliness in one way or another, women as different from one another as Campbell's wife Shelagh, founder of the Lydia Fellowship,[6] and Mary Pytches, wife of Bishop David Pytches, widely regarded himself as a father to many. These women have awakened in me a desire to emulate them, to pursue wisdom and integrity as they have done, and to grow old gracefully as they are doing. They have discovered the Father's love, and lost the never-ending need to live by earning the approval of others. It seems inconceivable that the mother of a baby should feel indifferent to the child's fate. Yet the Bible asks the question, 'Can a mother forget the baby at her breast and have no compassion on the child she has borne?' And answers, 'Though she may forget, I will not forget you!'[7] History as recorded through our newspapers testifies to the truth that blood relationship is insufficient to ensure love, protection and faithfulness. Far too often we open the newspapers only to read of terrible family conflicts that have ended in murder. The great majority of women who suffer rape suffer it at the hands of someone they know.

Other women who were not mothers of the flesh, such as Corrie ten Boom, the Dutchwoman who saw her sister die in a prisoner of war camp during the Second World War and years later famously expressed forgiveness to her German captors, also become role models for younger women. Gradually one comes to realise that marital status as a mother or father in the kingdom of God is almost inconsequential, whereas the wholehearted pursuit of God defines true biblical parenting. The brokenness of so many who are natural mothers and fathers, damaged by their own parents, and damaging in their turn their children, is in itself a clear call to every one of us to take up our mantle of mother or father to the next generation.

Today, church growth theorists, evangelists and missiologists increasingly segment communities and congregations into groups defined as Baby Boomers, Xers, and most recently, Millennials. In this they are following a growing number of social commentators and marketing experts who have sought to divide society along generational lines and to target different generational groups. They in turn reflect evolving legislation that, while purportedly acting to protect children and young people, in fact distances them subtly from their parents. A good example of this was the 1994 Declaration of the Rights of the Child. A more recent example is the Europe-wide legislation surrounding the subject of discipline in the home, which entitles a child/adolescent of 14 to appeal to the law should her parents attempt to impose sexual discipline. A more effective way of promoting family division would be hard to invent. The teenager struggling to emerge from the chrysalis of childhood could feel encouraged to drive a much bigger wedge through the web of family relationships if he has the law on his side.

In addition we are witnessing the appearance of fearful imbalance in generational statistics. As President Bush was inaugurated for his second term of office at the beginning of 2005, he promised to restore the crumbling pension scheme of his country. Why is it crumbling? Because in 1950, 15 working adults covered the pension of one retired adult; today, two working adults cover the pension of one retired one, and by 2010, there will be seven retired adults for every three working ones. Obviously no law could ever be sufficient to be the sole agent of solving this problem. Something needs to happen in the soul of a nation if we are not to see increasing numbers of the elderly physically and financially isolated.

Just as the proportion of those living well into their eighties has increased, and North America can expect 300,000 people over 100 to be alive in 2015, the respect accorded the elders in many cultures has steadily diminished. This is reflected in many spheres; for example, the market place. There is reluctance to employ anyone seeking to return to work after an absence should they have clocked up as many as 50 years, particularly women who have chosen to be home-based during the child-rearing years. Just as disturbing though is the disappearance of respect out in the street. My elderly mother and father lived on a quiet estate for six years, but were increasingly upset and intimidated by sporadic bouts of verbal aggression from children as young as ten who roamed through their street at all times of the day and night.

A further contributing factor to the distancing between generations is the dramatic acceleration of technology that has opened previously unparalleled access to information and travel for young adults. In addition the Xers' philosophy is post-modern and without absolutes. Knowledge and money are power, and combine to further dispel any remaining sense of rightful dependency on elders that was at one time the norm. In his book, *Devil's Advocate*,[8] John Humphrys addresses this disappearing sense of mutual responsibility. He argues that, in the brief span of some 50 years, Britain has turned from courage and self-sacrifice to compensation and self-indulgence. He illustrates this by contrasting the noble response to and rescue operation for the Aberfan Colliery disaster of 1969, with the very different aftermath of the 1989 Hillsborough disaster. Here we read almost as much about rescuers claiming compensation and counselling for the trauma occasioned by their involvement as we did about the trauma suffered by bereaved families or injured individuals. Few would dispute that today we are a people who are consumed by our own welfare, success and comfort, or that we have become what Humphrys calls a victim culture. Shamefully, these attitudes are all too prevalent in the church, and perhaps this is one reason why she is the ready target of the media, and therefore widely scorned or considered irrelevant.

It is not only respect for elders that needs to be retrieved; those of us who are older must stop tut-tutting at what we see and hear, and ask instead how we should interpret the seeming disappearance of all restraint and modesty.

One way is to understand the generation born roughly between 1964–81, dubbed Generation X by Douglas Coupland. In his novel so titled, an argument between the narrator, Andy, and his 40-year-old boss, Martin, encapsulates the Xers' rejection of the Boomers because of the pain caused by perceived abandon: having in his youth espoused the Woodstock generation's desire to recover a spiritual dimension, Martin has sold out and become a middle manager in an advertising agency, where he is now devoted to promoting hamburgers.

Hey, Martin. . .put yourself in my shoes. Do you *really* think we enjoy having to work in that toxic waste dump in there. . .and then have to watch you chat with your yuppie buddies about

your gut liposuction all day while you secrete artificially sweet-
ened royal jelly here in Xanadu?. . .Or for that matter do you
really think we enjoy hearing about your million-dollar home
when we're pushing thirty? A home you won in a genetic lot-
tery, I might add, sheerly by dint of your having been born at
the right time in history? You'd last about ten minutes if you
were my age these days, Martin. And I have to endure pin-
heads like you rusting above me for the rest of my life, always
grabbing the best piece of cake first and then putting a barbed-
wire fence around the rest. You really make me sick.[9]

The haemorrhage from the church is chiefly Generation X,
and we can see why if we care to look. Yet they are the most
likely to shape the form and direction of British society
in the early decades of the new millennium. Little wonder
then that the prevailing wind is blowing away from rather
than towards God, in ethical, legal or moral matters. Over
six million abortions have been performed in Britain since
David Steel's Abortion Law of 1967. Today we are on the
verge of following Holland and Belgium in legalising euthan-
asia. Where society is struggling to cater for increasing
numbers of people completing ten decades, no imagination
is necessary to envisage where this might lead. Legislation
is quietly advancing to make marriage no more than one
of a number of documents signifying an agreement to live
together. There are moves in the European Parliament to
further facilitate divorce, promote same-sex marriage and
parenting and give equal tax benefits and rights to any
cohabiting couple. Centuries ago, King Alfred drafted British Law beside an open Bible, and until 1917 British Lord
Chancellors had expressly stated that Christianity was part
and parcel of English Common Law. Since then we have all

but eradicated any trace of biblical content from our statute books.

All these things constitute a challenge and a clarion call to the church clearly to model a tri-generational, indeed increasingly a quadric-generational, community. We're called to heal generational rifts, to love and care for the elderly, to listen to and learn from the young; to respect the wisdom of the elders but not to despise the young. The Bible tells us that before darkness becomes so great on the earth that it leads to the dreadful day of the Lord, the hearts of the fathers will be turned to their children, and the hearts of the children to their fathers.[10] The darkness on earth was intensified by the Iraq War of 2003; nearly two years later they limped towards an election with the aim of re-establishing government by the Iraqi people, but the path was bloody; on a typical day in the run up to the election, BBC correspondent John Simpson reported the deaths of a police colonel and his five-year-old daughter; a judge and his son, and several civilians. On the same day another grim video of the most recent and still living hostage was broadcast on Al Jazeera. A surfeit of killing numbs the senses of the living as well as the dead. We think death cannot come near us but it did. . .in New York, in Madrid, in London. To process these things we have to rediscover our mortality here in the West; we have to find spiritual anchors and something bigger than our little lives.

What better place than in a multi-generational community where truths are handed down from generation to generation, lending security in an age of change? The Bible is a manifesto for intergenerational community, recounting failure as well as success.

Not only is generational unity written into the commandments, since the first commandment about human relationships is to honour our parents, but it is woven throughout the Scriptures. Moses instructs the Israelites:

> These commandments that I give you today are to be upon your hearts. Impress them on your children. Talk about them when you sit at home and when you walk along the road, when you lie down and when you get up. Tie them as symbols on your hands and bind them on your foreheads. Write them on the doorframes of your houses and on your gates.[11]

What goes around comes around, as they say, and while we find comic the idea of putting things on our foreheads, we still wear wristbands or badges to signal various allegiances. The well-known WWJD[12] bands drew criticism from some, yet they arise from the same principle; a desire to keep mindful of something. Make Poverty History's white wristbands carry the same message: Don't forget.

Many years ago we borrowed a caravan for our family holiday. With growing excitement and a certain unease between the parents, created by the responsibility of looking after something as large as a caravan, we drove sedately all the way to Cornwall. To our great consternation the entrance to the caravan site was a narrow gateway with large granite gateposts looking like some escaped menhirs from Stonehenge. Mounting excitement was replaced by tension in the front of the car, exacerbated by the now fractious and tired children in the back. We inched towards the ghastly gap, which seemed to narrow before our eyes, and words were reduced to sharp Shut-ups, and CAREFUL. . .all to no avail as an ugly rasping sound, caused by the caravan

coming into contact with the gatepost, struck our disbeliev-
ing ears, our hearts sank and our tempers boiled over. By
the time the caravan was in place, all six of us were in far
from what is often called a holiday mood. Opening the door
of the caravan for the first time, a display of stickers greeted
us: on every one was a verse from the Bible!

'Set a watch, O Lord before my mouth',[13] 'Be kind and
compassionate to one another, forgiving each other, just as
in Christ God forgave you.'[14]

Hmmm! We weren't very impressed and we did not
appreciate the décor, but wait a minute. . .it did remind us
of something; and it did defuse what could have continued
degenerating, given the fatigue and the frayed tempers we
were all displaying.

Over 400 years later, David proclaims the same message
as Moses:

> I'll let you in on the sweet old truths, stories we heard from our
> fathers, counsel we learned at our mother's knee. We're not
> keeping this to ourselves, we're passing it along to the next
> generation—God's fame and fortune, the marvellous things he
> has done. He planted a witness in Jacob, set his word firmly in
> Israel, then commanded our parents to teach it to their children
> so the next generation would know, and all the generations to
> come—know the truth and tell the stories so their children can
> trust in God. . .[15]

Elsewhere he says, 'future generations will be told about
the Lord. They will proclaim his righteousness to a people
yet unborn. . .'[16]

This is a theme dear to David, who had suffered a
generational breakdown between his predecessor, Saul, and

himself, caused by Saul's jealousy of David's friendship with
his son Jonathan, but also of David's abilities and prowess
in war. Jealousy is perhaps the greatest threat to intergenerational peace and harmony, for the success of a
younger person can provoke the irrational feeling that
being older we must be wiser or know better; but wisdom
comes from the knowledge of God. It is not for the sake of
it that Paul tells Timothy not to let people look down on
him because he was young.[17] It is because he knows that
Timothy has great wisdom and leadership gifts, nurtured by
Paul himself. He encourages Timothy to use the gifts of
preaching and teaching that he has. The text clearly states
that these gifts were given through a prophetic message
when the elders prayed for him.[18] This speaks of encouragement and releasing from the generation of his father.
However there is another reason that Timothy has much
wisdom at a young age. Writing that he misses him, Paul
mentions Timothy's faith: 'And what a rich faith it is,
handed down from your grandmother to your mother
Eunice and now to you.'[19]

Clearly David's priority of passing on the faith succeeded
with his son Solomon, who emphatically delivers the same
message in his writings. According to the prologue of
Proverbs:

> These are the wise sayings of Solomon. . .written down so we'll
> know how to live well and right. . .a manual for living, for
> learning what's right and just and fair; to teach the inexperi-
> enced the ropes and give our young people a grasp on reality.[20]

There are frequent references to 'my son(s)' which empha-
sise instructing the young so that they know how to become

wise and avoid pitfalls, but although it is a practical guide to living, reverence for God and reliance on him are clearly the baseline that makes this possible.

In a multi-cultural, multi-faith culture, the stories of God's dealings with man are no longer standard fare for a child's education; we can't even assume that the name of Jesus is familiar. On the other hand, an example of what is rapidly becoming standard fare is a homework exercise for eleven-year-olds that requires them to go out and practise buying condoms from the chemist.[21] Bothered? You should be.

So more than ever the church must be a source of learning and wisdom, and a shelter for the lonely and the disorientated. As the family slowly breaks down, there is an ever greater call for mothers and fathers to parent a lost generation.

The increasing breakdown of the marriage-based family is leaving an ever-widening wake of human suffering and social chaos. Drug abuse is now out of control. The media glorify sexual license, violence and obscene and blasphemous language. Degrading pornography has become a major industry, promiscuity is actively promoted and sexually-transmitted diseases are racing out of control. Vandalism has become a national disease. . .and there is widespread fear because of growing violence and lawlessness on our streets. . .Human relationships are increasingly presented. . .as temporary, valueless and dispensable, vast numbers of children have been deprived of family life, and especially of their fathers. . .we have robbed our children of their innocence. . .we have poisoned their minds by what they see, by what they read and what they hear. . .we have allowed them to be abused, corrupted and exploited. . .[22]

Statistics tell their own story: in the UK, 60,000 children live in care, 98 per cent of them admitted due to family breakdown;[23] over 110,000 adults have convictions for sex offences against children;[24] 100,000 children run away from home every year;[25] nearly 1.3 million children now have parents with addiction problems;[26] there were 846 abductions and attempted abductions of children in Britain in 2002–3, up from 584 the previous year;[27] the UK has the highest rate of teenage pregnancy in Europe, 40 per cent higher than Portugal in second place;[28] the number of 15-year-olds suffering from anxiety and depression has increased by 70 per cent since the mid 80s;[29] children as young as six are being treated for alcohol abuse, with one hospital reporting 'hundreds' of children admitted every week;[30] 156,000 young people become homeless in Britain each year.[31]

That's just the beginning; that's just the children; but statistics soon numb our faculties; as with the colossal numbers of tsunami victims, we wonder what we can do.

Well, God is seeking parents who are like him. You may not be a biological parent, but you can be a parent; this isn't my idea. . .it's in the Bible:

> Sing, O barren woman, you who never bore a child; burst into song, shout for joy, you who were never in labour; because more are the children of the desolate woman than of her who has a husband, says the Lord.[32]

God is calling us to be fathers and mothers to the next generation. While some will grow up in homes that welcome Jesus, many will not, and they need spiritual parenting, as Mike Bickle's words suggest. They desperately need as role models those who live out of knowing who they are in God, in other words gaining the mind of Christ, and becoming 'fully mature adults, fully developed within and without, fully alive like Christ. No prolonged infancies among us please. . .God wants us to grow up, to know the whole truth and tell it in love—like Christ in everything.'[33]

Every generation has its Simeons and Annas who are soaked in the presence of God, who know his love for them. What better aspiration could we have than to be like the barren woman in Isaiah, to whom God himself grants fruitfulness; and like Simeon who was righteous and devout, and who had the Holy Spirit on him? Do you long to be at ease with every generation? Does your heart yearn for parents or for children? Pursue God with all your being, and search out the people of God. Whatever your situation and status as you read this, it is your destiny to be connected with grandparents, parents and children, whichever of the three you are, and to give and receive healing as you form the community of God's people where you live.

My Big Fat Greek Wedding and *Monsoon Wedding* are two films that unintentionally visualise this destiny. Both are full of movement, colour and laughter, and portray the whole gamut of emotions belonging to the complex web of family relationships. I am privileged to be reminded of the glory of family destiny every Sunday morning at St Aldate's. As we begin the service, there is a wonderful time of holy chaos, as swarms of little children crowd onto the stage with all their helpers and teachers and the whole church sings a couple of worship songs. I confess I'm often laughing at the antics of the children rather than worshipping! There are some who stare into space, some who scowl, some who wriggle, some who make loud remarks. . . and some who sing: but if I were an angel, leaning over heaven's balustrade, I would be looking at the bride of Christ dressed to make his heart beat fast with passionate love as he sees one generation tell another.

5

Simeons and Samuels, Hannahs and Annas

The destiny of prayer

More things are wrought by prayer than this world dreams of.
(Tennyson)

In November 2003, police found the body of an 18-year-old girl in a remote spot on Dartmoor. She had been missing for nine days. The nation had watched the unfolding of a far too familiar sequence. First there were high hopes that the missing teenager would be found. After all, she was not returning home foolishly late at night. No, she was walking along the country lanes in the morning to catch the bus that would take her to college. Then anxiety was publicly acknowledged. There was a possibility that this might become a murder hunt. And it did, with the grim discovery on the rocky hillside. A 39-year-old bus driver was charged with her murder. That young girl, whose name was Alicia, will never have the chance to fulfil her destiny.

Alicia's name is no longer familiar to us, but it was for a

short time. Just over a year earlier, the nation had reeled as the equally tragic story of Holly Wells and Jessica Chapman was played out before us. Two more children of destiny savagely picked off. Like Alicia, the girl from Dartmoor, Holly and Jessica will never live out the lives they were born for.

However, such terrible events, of which these are but two examples among many more, are in one sense the tip of the iceberg. Across the nation, untold numbers of parents, many of them Christians, are also silently suffering at the disappearance of their children. These children are not physically dead, but they are dead to spiritual realities and every choice they make takes them further from the light. The less light they have, the more they risk making poor decisions as a result of impaired vision. To see the next generation enter into the destiny prepared for them we need to understand what it means to be provoked to prayer, and respond by learning what it means to pray with desperation and urgency.

Stories like those of Alicia and Holly and Jessica sound a faint alarm signal in us, but rarely do we engage in persistent prayer for those we don't know. We are more likely to be numbed. But occasionally danger comes closer.

We experienced something of the utter terror that grips one's being at the possibility that a child is missing and in danger during our time in Paris. One day I came home to our flat in Paris to be greeted by Alice blurting out that she didn't know where Hannah was. The school had phoned to enquire about her absence since the next day her A-Level Art Exhibition was due to be examined, but it was not even hung. Fearing the wrath of her parents (but also succumbing to the crushing accusation of failure), Hannah had taken off. As the realisation dawned that I had no idea where she was, a sickening contraction seized my stomach, the same physical reaction to the events of Samuel's death years earlier. Control had been snatched from my hands. A blinding panic invaded my senses as my vivid imagination went into overdrive. There was nothing I could do to retrieve Hannah. Or was there?

Coincidentally, or perhaps by a larger design, our friend John Mulinde was making one of his visits to Paris. He had been due to address the elders of the church that evening, but came instead to our house to pray with and for us, since Charlie, distraught, had telephoned to cancel the meeting.

'There is only one thing you can do in a situation like this, and that is to pray,' he said in his quiet but authoritative voice. We had learned from John how they had learned to pray in situations of desperation under the reigns of Idi Amin and Milton Obote. We had heard him tell of babies bayoneted at road checkpoints and of family members disappearing; we had heard how, confronted by an anarchy and violence beyond our comprehension, the Christians had turned to prayer. And we had heard of God's answers to their cries and of miraculous interventions that turned the nation around. We sensed that there was a power and authority in the prayers flowing out of John and his friend Enos.

We had listened to many teachings on prayer and read a number of books on the subject, but we learned far more that afternoon as we experienced being at the mercy of God, and far removed from an academic exercise. We begged and pleaded with God that he would return our daughter to us. We did not have to think about the composition of our prayers, and eloquence was the last thing on our minds. We and our other children knelt on the floor and wept uncontrollably, uttering our desperation, while the steady voices of John and Enos called out to the God they knew and trusted and had seen respond in far more tragic situations in their own country.

Hannah's return, her subsequent healing from the demands of this strange Parisian existence, and our realisation that we had not really understood the inner pressures she experienced during this troubled time are recounted in Charlie's book, *The Discipline of Intimacy*.[1]

God is calling us to desperate prayer and in his wisdom he sometimes allows us to realise our dependence on him by not relieving our circumstances as quickly as we would like. God allows our lives to take certain turns because his heart is longing for intimacy with us. He cannot force us. One of the best expressions of this truth was penned by C. S. Lewis in the timeless classic *The Screwtape Letters*, in a correspondence from a senior demon to his nephew instructing him how to be most effective in seducing people away from their Creator and Saviour:

> You must have often wondered why the enemy [God] does not make more use of his power to be sensibly present to human souls in any degree he chooses and at any moment. But you now see that the irresistible and the indisputable are the two weapons which the very nature of his scheme forbids him to use. Merely to over-ride a human will (as his felt presence in any but the faintest and most mitigated degree would certainly do) would be for him useless. He cannot ravish. He can only woo. For his ignoble idea is to eat the cake and have it; the creatures are to be one with him, but yet themselves; merely

to cancel them, or assimilate them, will not serve. . .Sooner or later he withdraws, if not in fact, at least from their conscious experience, all supports and incentives. He leaves the creature to stand up on its own legs—to carry out from the will alone duties which have lost all relish. . .He cannot 'tempt' to virtue as we do to vice. He wants them to learn to walk, and must therefore take away his hand. . .Our cause is never more in danger than when a human, no longer desiring, but still intending, to do our enemy's will, looks round upon a universe from which every trace of him seems to have vanished, and asks why he has been forsaken, and still obeys.[2]

Many of us, in our pain, have detached from our wayward sons and daughters, committing them to the mercies of God. While that is admirable, it is not enough. God is looking for a people who will 'stand up on their own legs' and engage doggedly with him where pain has removed desire. He is looking for a people who will press in on behalf of prodigals though they feel utterly forsaken, who will plead with him on behalf of the next generation and who will not rest until they see the fruit of their prayers.

One of the things that deters us in our pursuit of prayer is God's apparent deafness and silence; why, if we choose to pray with perseverance and discipline, do we not see what we are seeking sooner? The answer is that God provokes us to prayer by withholding the answer, not only for the development of our character but also because the answer must fit into his timing. This is because the answer is always much bigger than we realise. Our children will decide to follow Jesus, not for themselves alone, and not simply to assure themselves of a place in heaven, but for the village they live in, or the college at which they are a student, or the workplace they will one day be in. Some of them will become leaders in the city and some leaders in the nation. Some will be prophets, some will be priests and many will be worshippers who lead the people of God into his presence. Today God is searching out those who will be steadfast in prayer for them, trusting him in the dark. I think that he is calling many of us who have laid down our arms out of pain and exhaustion to pick them up again and resume our partnership of prayer with him.

Of the four intercessors who name this chapter, I've chosen to look more closely at Hannah, whose prayer, when it was answered, would change the historical course of the nation of Israel. Here was a woman who, when we meet her, knew nothing of this, but only the suffering of barrenness and the ignominy it brought. In Old Testament times, barrenness was considered to be a judgement from God that brought shame, and Peninnah, Hannah's rival, kept provoking her because of it. The story in 1 Samuel chapter 1 relates that it was God who had closed her womb, and brought this shameful sterility upon her. The received idea that somehow this was meant by God, indicating divine disfavour and legitimising social reproach and mockery, drove Hannah to desperate prayer for deliverance. She was literally provoked to prayer, as many of us should be, but somehow there is often a veil over our understanding, and we relinquish our determination to press on. We fall prey to the idea that somehow this is what we deserve, and the pain of waiting slowly robs us of hope; energy drains from our spirit and our call to God grows fainter and fainter.

All of us at one time or another will need an inner strength to tackle the suffering we encounter. I do not know any parent who has been spared pain in relation to a child or children. What can we learn from the example of Hannah to set our feet on a rock when the storm rages?

First of all I believe she had a longing, and this longing was so strong that at a certain moment it broke into the downward spiral and something inside her snapped. The text says, 'Once when they had finished eating and drinking. . .'[3] What happened at that meal? Was Peninnah indulging in her sport of mocking Hannah? Was Hannah devouring with her eyes Peninnah's offspring, seated around the table, noisily laughing and talking to one another? Was she observing the powerful affection between father and children? Was the painful reality that none of these lively children were the fruit of her intimacy with Elkanah burning into her more than usual? Was she reflecting on how another year had passed and here they were at Shiloh again with everyone asking for news, and she had none? Perhaps it was a mixture of all these things, but whatever it was, the key is that the longing had more power than the despair. What longings do you have, buried beneath your present circumstances?

I remember the intense longing for a son that grew in me all those years ago. It was not like Hannah's in that it was not birthed out of barrenness. But I believe it came from God and was connected to his purpose in birthing the next generation. At the time I had no idea that, 20 years later, I would have developed a passion for and understanding of the purposes of God through this generation. Of course I had no idea of all that lay before us in the political and technological arenas, and of how that might affect my perspective concerning the call upon the next generation. Likewise,

Hannah had no idea that her son would be God's instrument to identify and anoint David king and thus affect the history of her nation. She had no idea that her son would be the one to reconnect the nation with God. Despite the religious festivals, the book of Samuel records that in those days the word of the Lord was rare; there were not many visions.

Secondly, Hannah was authentic. She didn't conceal her bitterness from God. She didn't apparently feel the need to clothe herself in a religious garment before approaching God. I remember someone, many years ago, describing her feeling of unworthiness in the presence of God in the following terms: 'I skulked around the kitchen, hoping I wouldn't bump into God.' We are so often like this. The idea of earning a hearing is so deep within us. But not Hannah. In bitterness of soul she wept much and prayed to the Lord. She was not only weeping, but, the text tells us twice, not eating. Was she fasting? I don't think she had planned a fast to coincide with this spiritual pilgrimage. Not only does the text not use the word, but the festival they were attending was in all probability the Feast of Tabernacles, commemorating God's care for his people during the desert journey to the Promised Land, and celebrating with joy and feasting God's blessing on the year's crops. The emphasis on fruitfulness would have made the whole event yet more poignantly painful for Hannah. Because it was a feast, not a fast, it is unlikely that Hannah determined to act in a way which would have drawn attention to her plight. Clearly, Peninnah upset her so much on these occasions that she was reduced to tears and lost her appetite. She lost her appetite because the subject of her torment, her childlessness, mattered to her so deeply. Her whole being cried out to God, so in a sense she *was* fasting, because her hunger for God outweighed her physical hunger.

I believe that God is calling his church, perhaps especially in the indulgent, overfed Western world, back to the spiritual discipline of fasting; back to the possibility that time in his presence to nourish our soul far outweighs the short-lived pleasure of satisfying our flesh.

Thirdly, Hannah connected emotionally. She did not try to present a clearly thought out idea to God. She did not have a project, she just had pain and longing, and she probably couldn't have explained it if she had been asked. The text suggests that she wasn't very collected or prepared, other than in the ongoing story of her heart, and I think God is waiting for us to cross the religious boundary and pour out our hearts to him in a similar way today.

The book of Romans says that the Holy Spirit helps us in our weakness, that we do not know what we ought to pray for, but that the Spirit himself intercedes for us with groans that words cannot express (Romans 8:26). Likewise the author of Hebrews tells us that during the days of Jesus' life on earth, he offered up prayers and petitions with loud cries and tears to the One who could save him from death, and he was heard because of his reverent submission.[4] These two texts show us several things. First, that being emotionally in command of ourselves is not the key to being heard by God. Second, that to abandon ourselves to God in our grief or desperation or ignorance simply gives the Holy Spirit room to help us. Third, that to pray silently or quietly is not necessarily an indication of submission. All these things add up to what the Bible calls being filled with the

Spirit. Hannah was connected with God; she knew she was making contact and Eli's blessing confirmed it. E. M. Bounds writes:

> We pray not by the truth the Holy Spirit reveals to us, but we pray by the actual presence of the Holy Spirit. He puts the desire in our hearts; kindles the desire by his own flame. We simply give lip and voice and heart to his unutterable groanings.[5]

Fourthly, part of the strength of the longing within her was that it freed her from the tyranny of social conventions. She would have known that it was not unusual for drunken people to enter the Temple, but she was not put off by the possibility of being misunderstood. As indeed she turned out to be. She was not apparently embarrassed by Eli's interjection, but answered calmly. Her reply, that she had not been drinking but that she was pouring out her soul to God and praying out of her great anguish and grief, in other words, that she was engaging with God about a personal situation, clearly had the authority to reassure Eli, who gave her his blessing. I have pondered those words of Eli's over and over again: 'Go in peace and may the God of Israel grant you what you have asked of him.'[6] I am sure that as he spoke them, Hannah knew that a heavenly transaction had taken place. Eli, after all, represented God, and in the days of the Old Testament priesthood, he carried the Lord's presence as mediator of his grace. I am sure that Hannah returned home from Shiloh with a sense of peace and release to resume what had hitherto been rather fraught intimate relations with Elkanah.

How do we find this sense of peace and certainty today,

now that we have personal access to God through the cruci-
fixion of Jesus on our behalf and no longer need a mediator?
I think it comes from knowing that we too have left behind
social conventions and allowed the real burden of our being
to be expressed in the raw. We may not hear words of blessing such as those pronounced by Eli, but we may find a word
from the Bible suddenly becoming three-dimensional.

I remember this happening with the words that Elizabeth
spoke prophetically to Mary at that wonderful meeting of
the two expectant mothers, one well along in years (which
might mean anything upwards of 25) and the other barely
a teenager: 'Blessed is she who has believed that what the
Lord has said to her will be accomplished.'[7] They bore
meaning for me, not about Samuel, but concerning an opportunity I believed the Lord would one day give me as a
teacher.

Fifthly, Hannah was rash. In her desperation, she made a
vow. She promised that if God gave her a son she would
give him back to God for his whole life. She made a vow on
behalf of this child that he would be set apart for God all the
days of his life. Did she realise the implications of her
prayer, one of which would be that she would not see much
of him once he was about three years old? In the form of
prayer we use for a Dedication Service, there is a question
to the parents:

> 'If God were to call X or Y to a life of great service or sacrifice,
> would you gladly consent and give your blessing?'

God is looking for this kind of dedication, by parents of
children, and there are many who might hear his call to re-
dedicate their prodigal children all over again, in the secret

place of prayer. A verse in the book of Chronicles says that the eyes of the Lord range throughout the earth to strengthen those whose hearts are fully committed to him.[8] If we are reckless in trusting him with the things that matter most to us, we will be strengthened and see answers as glorious as the birth of Samuel.

Sixthly, Hannah had a secret history with God. Though everybody in her entourage obviously knew her situation and her sorrow, they were unaware of the inside story between Hannah and her God. Her outburst in the Temple was not an isolated incident between them, but a glimpse we are privileged to observe of a well developed relationship. She did not suddenly think of the idea of vowing to give the fruit of her womb back to God. Too often our friendship with God is aired on a Sunday, or when storm clouds are gathering, but God searches for constant rather than intermittent connection, for friendship such as he enjoyed with Moses or Abraham. The intimacy of such relationships leads to the kind of desperate prayer that we have seen in the story of Hannah. Today God is stirring up his people to rediscover this same intimacy that is birthed in our secret history, that's to say our personal story with him, and that opens the way to a connection in prayer that unlocks heaven and thus prepares the way for revival. You and I must grasp the amazing consequences arising from friendship with God.

The seeds of our move to Paris were being planted. Very early in 1989, a friend had invited me to spend a weekend in Paris with her to celebrate both our birthdays. She had found a cheap deal and, having never been on a plane, decided this was the moment. I agreed on condition that we visit a church in the east of the city that we had heard of through friends. To this day, the impact of the smells, the noise, the bustle, the colour and the sheer buzz as we emerged from the metro at the bottom of the Rue de Belleville, remains as vivid as it was then. I took a deep breath, and exclaimed excitedly to my friend, but inside I was saying, 'Oh God, I know that I know that I know that I want to live here among these people of many nations; I know that we must come and live here. . .' My ribcage felt as if it would explode, so intense was the certainty that I was standing in the very arrondissement that would be my future home. Simultaneously, my friend burst out, 'How disgusting! What an awful, dirty place. . .just look at the pavement!'

Some weeks later, driving to Chelmsford to go shopping, I came to a tree-lined part of the road that always reminded me of a French route nationale, and suddenly heard the words, 'You will certainly go and live in France.' It is the only occasion when I think I have heard an audible voice from God, and that incident fortified me for the interval of three years that was to elapse before we did move to Paris. A secret history builds confidence for the storms, the desperate times and the times of waiting.

Finally, Hannah co-operated in the natural realm. In other words, she and Elkanah made love. Perhaps a new confidence took the tension out of their intimacy and all the fears previously associated with what God intends to be pleasurable and fun. This is the paradox of intensity in our dealings with God. If we allow our suffering and trials to provoke us to prayer and perseverance rather than despair, we will grow in confidence that he is for us not against us, and that we are encountering not silence but the timing and purposes of God. While my main focus is the next generation, all the principles outlined in this book apply to every longing generated by all kinds of sterility. We may long for marriage, or for a child, or for a fruitful ministry, or for healing, or for a host of other things. We may long for reconciliation with someone, or that we might overcome a violent temper or a paralysing timidity. In each case the Father makes his wooing call that we would not give up, but grow up by choosing to persevere.

If we are thinking of urgent prayer for the next generation, provoked in our spirits by an understanding of the enemy's plan to neutralise if not destroy them, how can we co-operate in the natural realm? Rob Parsons, in his excellent book *Bringing Home the Prodigals*,[9] challenges the church to acknowledge that there are as many prodigals inside the church as outside. His thesis is that often we have cared more about the length of their skirts, the colour of their hair and their attendance at the youth group than about their passion for the poor or their search for integrity and authenticity.

The summer after we returned to England, a friend whom we much loved died. His funeral was one of the most moving I have ever attended. It was very informal, washed in tears, and all his children, children-in-law and grandchildren took part, even if one or two of the little ones were too overcome once on the stage in front of all those people to do what was planned. My mind went back to the uncompromising stance of liberty that these parents had granted their teenagers years earlier. Not liberty in moral or ethical areas, but freedom, for example, to dress how they pleased, as teenagers will, however crazy they looked. They had refused to constrict their children in order to win approval from others for themselves, and I remember admiring them for it. Now, in these children at their father's funeral, I saw young men and women living their destiny. Death had brought them grief, but not confusion or defeat.

Our call is to follow our children's lead in the pursuit of content rather than style, in their rejection of superficiality and search for authenticity. It is to encourage them to explore what they feel they are called for, not to manoeuvre them towards the life we wished we had lived now that we can see a bit more clearly. It is to express approval at every opportunity, to show them respect and to listen to them carefully. It is to give them as much freedom as we can. If we do these things we will know how to pray for them, and the destiny stored up for them in heaven will be unlocked as we allow desperation to provoke us to persevering on their behalf.

6

Slowing Down and Sweetening Up

The destiny of friendship

It redoubleth joys, and cutteth griefs in halves.
(Francis Bacon)

Tears streaming down my face, I painstakingly tapped out my message: 'not copng, pls pry. A'. I pressed 'send' and watched the little envelope rapidly zigzagging away to the corner of my mobile phone. Two minutes later, back came the reply: 'am pryng, will rng lter, lve you. J'. That day was a Sunday, and my struggles to acclimatise to a new role in a huge church were proving overwhelming. Suddenly the thought of being on view again while my emotions were in such turmoil was all too much and, dissolving in tears, I had told Charlie that I wasn't going to church; and none too gently at that. Now, in addition to sobs wracking my body, I was feeling guilty and a failure for giving in and giving up, albeit temporarily. But as the little beep announced the arrival of a message, the knot in my stomach miraculously dissolved and relief from pain stole into my weary being.

Friendship is a divine institution, and it is God's intention that each of us has a number of people whom we count as intimate friends. Indeed the root meaning of the word intimacy has to do with deep and close friendship rather than having a sexual connotation as it tends to today. Friendship used to evolve naturally through the community based society, but the technological revolution of the latter part of the twentieth century has ensured that with the dissolution of a community has come immeasurable loneliness. Henri Nouwen captures this well in his book, *Seeds of Hope:*

> What most strikes me, being back in the United States, is the full force of the restlessness, the loneliness and the tension that holds so many people. The conversations I had today were about spiritual survival. So many of my friends feel overwhelmed by the many demands made on them. . . To celebrate life together, to be together in community, to simply enjoy the beauty of creation, the love of people and the goodness of God—those seem faraway ideals.[1]

I remember being told just prior to going to live in Paris in 1992 that 75 per cent of the Parisian population lived alone, a fact mirrored in the make-up of the church we had gone there to serve. Many things testify to the loneliness of our culture, from the despair that can lead to suicide to the avalanche of lonely hearts adverts to be found in any newspaper, periodical or magazine. Many seek to flee such unbearable loneliness through finding a sexual partner, which is why the vast majority of such advertisements announce a very desirable person seeking a very exciting person, sometimes very explicitly. Yet what so often lies beneath the appearance is the longing for friendship.

Many are the testimonies of how God has taken a wilderness experience and transformed it into a school of discipleship, to hone the character for the good works he has prepared in advance for us to do.[2] In these times the comfort and encouragement of a friend can be the difference between pressing on to take hold of that for which Christ Jesus took hold of me[3] or giving into temptations that come from our self-pity and lead us to comforting ourselves in other ways, with food, alcohol, drugs or sex. A more serious source of comfort that is contemporary is the increasing practice of self-harm. For some, the external pain is more bearable, indeed preferable, to the pain inside and for others, the sight of blood is evidence of life and creates a feeling of reality. A local news item recently highlighted the case of a woman whose depression had led to cutting herself: 'The pain inside would gradually get worse until I could hardly bear it. As soon as I drew blood, the relief came; I felt real again.'

Any of these false comforters can lead to slavery. And slavery, as Paul notes in Romans 7, is notoriously difficult to escape from. He describes something we are all so familiar with: being motivated to do right and finding ourselves doing the exact opposite: wrong.

Studies show that the average number of people we can relate to in a meaningful way is 6 to 12 intimates, 24 to 30 maintained friendships and up to 200 acquaintances. The speed of travel and communications and the emergence of the global village have ensured that we all have far in excess of 200 acquaintances. Many of us know we cannot manage the number of people we 'know' and develop different ways of handling what is in some senses an insoluble problem. We live on adrenalin or substances, or we neglect and eventually lose former friendships. Yet we are designed to walk through life hand in hand with our family and friends. Friends restore perspective, reassure us that we are going in the right direction, and hold us in the dark nights of our life.

Such was my experience all those years ago when Samuel died, and all colour and hope drained out of my being. Any tragedy is a bleak moment, a moment of choice, and a moment when those observing might hold their breath: this could go either way. Stuart and Celia were there for Charlie and me. They were there with tears, with laughter, with tea, with wine, with their bodies to hug us and transfer warmth where there was creeping coldness. They were there with the organising of our days, with suggestions of things to do, with the gift of sending us away for those days in Carmel and looking after the girls. In short they were there in thought, word and deed.

The Bible has plenty to say about friendship, and a touching example of this sort of close friendship is found in the relationship between David and Jonathan. When Saul realises that the young David is far more popular than him, a jealous fury is aroused in him, and from being pleased with David, and liking him very much,[4] this jealousy provokes him to make attempts on David's life. Although Jonathan is Saul's son, his loyalties lie with David. They have entered into a covenant relationship; in other words a friendship that nothing can destroy, based on love and mutual respect. Jonathan helps David escape from Saul, and though they can no longer enjoy one another's company, their friendship endures.

'Jonathan said to David, "Go in peace, for we have sworn friendship with each other in the name of the Lord, saying 'The Lord is witness between you and me, and between your descendants and my descendants forever.'"'[5]

I believe this is God's blueprint for intimate friendship: that it is covenantal and that it is life-long. There is a call to us to invest in and nurture such friendships, not only for ourselves but to model a disappearing facet of societal life to others. Some of our friendships are seasonal however. Circumstances bring one near to people, but later they change and a relationship that was at one time closely maintained gradually becomes more distant. Many relationships are simply hung up in a Christmas card once a year, and that's the way it has to be. There is no fault attached. But for each of us, a few friendships survive these circumstantial changes, and indeed are strengthened by them.

Intimate friends are the ones you can say anything to. The ones to whom you can confess your failures and your fears, your hopes and your dreams. True friends are also those who have the right to confront you: 'Wounds from a friend can be trusted, but an enemy multiplies kisses.'[6]

Recently we travelled up north to visit some friends we have known for at least 20 years. It had been very difficult to arrange the trip for all sorts of reasons but it was good to have finally made it. Soon after arriving, though, we found ourselves in what could have been a difficult conversation, revolving around the question of whether we were really committed to them, since they felt they were always having to take the initiative. Explanations and assurances followed, and we had three wonderful days together, catching up at a deep level after a long absence. We came away strengthened in our friendship and grateful to have a relationship with no no-go areas.

In her book *Between Friends*, Mary Pytches speaks about this level of transparency being crucial for any life-long friendship, illustrating her point with stories of her friendship with Prue Bedwell, with whom she spent many years in ministry. For many of us this is an intimidating notion, because we have absorbed as if by osmosis the cultural norm of non-interference and relativism ('you do your thing, I'll do mine'). This means that the stuff of real relationships—what the Bible calls speaking the truth in love,[7] or being honest—is rare.

Another reason for the scarcity of inspiring models of friendship is the absence of natural community where friendship can automatically grow. We are a commuting people, and increasingly this begins with our school years, so that we grow up with little expectation of forging close friendships by the time we embark on tertiary education or go out into the workplace. In turn this leads to ineptitude in the social skills necessary for the cultivating of friendships. We have been amazed at the number of encounters we have had in a social setting at which we have not been asked one single question!

The opportunity to share our experiences and debrief from our work remains a vital need for every one of us, so if a vacuum is created through lack of community we will instinctively search it out elsewhere. As already suggested, the lonely hearts columns bear witness to this, but another forum for contact is the increasingly big business of counselling. While fully supportive of all forms of professional and attested counselling (and having myself been involved in counselling for many years), I am nevertheless persuaded that a proportion of counselling arises from loneliness that has overtaken a person to the point where they are no longer fully in command of their behaviour. While much of this stems from what is commonly referred to as a dysfunctional family environment, it is exacerbated by a barren field where friendship is concerned. It is now rare, if you are having trouble with your parents or your boss or your spouse, to be able to pour out your woes to a person in whom you have tried and tested confidence; someone who will talk you down from your cliffs, restore perspective, offer both a challenge (are you over-reacting?) and wisdom. It is rare to find someone who you can be sure will not repeat your sorrows to another, and who will often prevent a crisis caused by decisions taken in the heat of the moment.

Almost every week of our ten years in Paris, we met with our co-pastors, a German-Swiss and French-Swiss couple. Despite the considerable cultural differences, we lived a true friendship, laughing together, crying together, questioning each other and comforting each other. It wasn't always easy, and there were misunderstandings from time to time. But all of us were committed to each other and loved each other (as we still do!) and would take the time and the pain necessary to unravel things and restore peace. Indeed we knew that in some senses our lives depended on it, for we were out of our comfort zones, with tasks that we often felt were beyond us. Perhaps it is the very availability of so many false comforts that lure us away from the effort of friendship building. A newsreader recently declared in a news item on Radio 4 that Britain is now so awash with narcotic goods that, 'a line of cocaine can cost as little as a cappuccino'.

The Bible furnishes many examples of close friendship. It calls Abraham God's friend[8] and recounts God confiding his plans to Abraham: 'Shall I hide from Abraham what I am about to do?[9] The marks of friendship here are trust, confidence and revelation; being certain of loyalty if we open our hearts is one of the highest forms of friendship, and something that encourages us (imparts courage) and builds us up (edifies us). True friendship can survive disagreement as the Sodom and Gomorrah incident that follows this choice to confide in Abraham illustrates. What God does not hide from Abraham is that he is on the verge of destroying these two cities because of their wickedness. Abraham engages God in a lively debate about the conditions under which the cities might escape destruction. As the story goes on to illustrate, our friends will not always do what we want them to, supremely so if the friend in question is God. Nevertheless, Abraham clearly remained God's friend despite the fate of Sodom and Gomorrah and there are several references to him as such throughout the Bible.[10]

Likewise, Moses is portrayed as a friend of God. Exodus 33 describes Moses going to the Tent of Meeting to speak with God. One can well imagine Moses' fluctuating emotions as he led the recalcitrant Israelites round and round the wilderness, and we know from other passages that he railed at God for ever giving him such a depressing job. But here we see the presence of God, manifested in the pillar of cloud, staying at the entrance to the tent while Moses is inside and the encounter is described as follows: 'The Lord would speak to Moses face to face, as a man speaks with his friend.'[11]

There is something about eye contact. The Bible tells us that the eye is the lamp of the body, and that if our eyes are good, our whole body will be full of light, but that if our eyes are bad, our whole body will be full of darkness.[12] Instinctively, we concur. A straight and steady gaze inspires confidence and suggests an openness and honesty, whereas we speak of a shifty look or stare which makes us suspicious. To avoid eye contact is a common sign of something being wrong, though whatever is wrong may be the result of another relationship or event. If darkness has entered our life at the hands of another, as in the case of a person who has suffered abuse, it can still be signalled through our eyes.

Early on in our time in Paris, I was called out of a service to see if I could help a young girl who had been brought to church by her mother. Sandra was not only avoiding eye contact, but her very eyes were invisible, covered by locks of dark and unkempt hair tumbling around her face. She was allowed to leave the psychiatric ward in which she passed the majority of her time for a few hours at the weekend. It was the beginning of a long story and an enduring friendship which, coupled with professional help, led to a full recovery; today Sandra is married and mother to a little girl.

The intimacy of friendship implies knowledge; familiarity with the way a person reflects and reacts, reasons and relates. Such friends to God were the prophets of the Old Testament, men and women who were familiar with God's law and character, but also with God's pain and suffering, as he watched his chosen people repeatedly turn away from his laws and betray him. These were the people who could warn of God's coming judgement but also tell of his mercy, confident in their knowledge and understanding of the nature of God. Amos even makes a point of this intimacy when he says: 'Surely the Sovereign Lord does nothing without revealing his plan to his servants the prophets.'[13]

Despite this, the sad story of the Old Testament is that the exhortations and warnings of the prophets went unheeded, and we are reminded of this as we hear Jesus, hundreds of years later, lamenting over it in the Temple: 'O Jerusalem, Jerusalem, you who kill the prophets and stone those sent to you, how often I have longed to gather your children together, as a hen gathers her chicks under her wings, but you were not willing.'[14]

Jesus supremely modelled friendship with his disciples. Indeed the very fact that he limited himself to twelve disciples reflects the truth that intimacy is only possible with a small number of people.

During the discussion between Jesus and the disciples at the Last Supper (more like a briefing for what was coming, though the disciples were not really up to speed), Jesus makes an interesting remark about friendship: 'I no longer call you servants, because a servant doesn't know his master's business. Instead I have called you friends, for everything that I learned from my Father, I have made known to you.'[15]

So friendship is about the inner circle, about inside knowledge. Here it's also about revelation; about growing in the knowledge of God. In the intimacy of a shared meal, Jesus is conveying information essential for knowing what to do when he's gone. But the content of the discussion also reveals that friendship with Jesus is to be the norm for every person who comes to believe in him, through the Holy Spirit. The Holy Spirit is the Spirit of truth, the presence of Jesus in spirit form, which will be available to every believer once the bodily Jesus has ascended to heaven following the Resurrection.

Just prior to this remark about friendship being to do with opening one's heart, Jesus has identified himself in another way as their friend: 'Greater love has no man than this; that he lay down his life for his friends. You are my friends if you do what I command [which is to love one another].'[16]

So friendship with God has to do with knowing him, obeying him and being willing to follow him anywhere, whatever the risks and cost; and by implication friendship with man also involves sacrifice.

Mike Bickle writes,

A deeply satisfied soul, a personal sense of meaning and significance and a rich treasure store of divine pleasure can only come through the intimate knowledge of God himself. . .Do you desire divine satisfaction beyond your greatest imaginations? Then focus on two things: first focus on the intimate knowledge of God's beauty, or what God looks like (in terms of knowing his personality). Second focus on the knowledge of what it means to be created in his image, in other words what we look like to God in Christ. . .imagine, the beauty Jesus possesses is the very beauty he imparts to his bride in the gift of righteousness.

Our ability to demonstrate real friendship on earth is related to the quality and depth of our relationship and friendship with our heavenly Father. How well do we know him? How well do we know his word? How well do we know how he thinks? What his plans and purposes are? What he thinks about men and women? What he thinks about creation?

What the meaning of stewardship is? What the Bible tells us about death? About heaven? The questions are endless, for God is infinite, his judgements are unsearchable, and his paths beyond tracing out.[17]

Not long ago, I sensed a renewed challenge from God: How well do you know my word? How familiar are you, after nearly 30 years of being my disciple, with the Bible? How confident are you in handling it? How quickly can you find a story, a proverb, a saying, a prophecy that comes to mind? Since that time I have redoubled my efforts to become intimate with the Bible. Not with my favourite passages, but with the whole counsel of God. The more I read, study and meditate, the more I am intrigued by the unfathomable yet approachable God I love, accessible through his long, lingering love-letter; the greater is my hunger to be more familiar every year with more of this living book, unique in being three-dimensional. I feel an urgency, an inner compulsion to become an ever more intimate friend of God. I know that to have a secret history with God is the surest route to wisdom and maturity, and the surest qualification for being a good friend to those God has given me to love.

Passion and love are caught more than taught and you get them from being around such people. Much of my passion for God, to know and meditate on God's word, has come through my long years of association with the Lydia Fellowship. The name is drawn from Acts 16, where we meet Lydia and discover two things about her; that she is an astute businesswoman and a worshipper of God. Interestingly, it is implied that to worship God is not a guarantee of knowing God, for after listening to Paul, she and the members of her household are baptised, a sign of beginning a new faith.

Lydia is also very hospitable, persuading Paul and his companions to stay at her home. Earlier in the chapter, Paul has received the vision of the Macedonian man, standing and begging him to come and help them. In Paul's visit to Lydia and her prayer group, we witness the momentous event of the gospel's arrival in Europe, in the city of Phillipi on the eastern shores of Greece.[18]

It was while reading this story that the Spirit of God spoke to Shelagh McAlpine's heart and the vision of a prayer movement was conceived. Today the Lydia Fellowship is an international, transdenominational network of women whose main objective is to mobilise this generation of Christians and the next worldwide to pray with fasting at least once a month for their church, their community, their country and nations of the world, through the establishing of prayer partnerships or small prayer cells. Nothing more and nothing less. The distinctives of Lydia are meditation on the word of God, so an ever-growing familiarity with the Bible; and time set apart to pray according to God's word, turning his word itself into prayer. It is a movement that beats with a strong missionary heart, full of compassion and placing a high value on relationships.

As a young woman, I was drawn by the perfume of many of these women. Not Chanel but Jesus. I couldn't get enough of their company and took every opportunity to listen to them, ask questions and soak up their wisdom; wisdom I knew found its source in the intimacy they enjoyed with God. Today many of them are also Annas, widowed for few or many long years, and full of grace and truth. Heaven only knows to what extent their prayers have brought mercy where we deserved to reap what we have sown.

The ups and downs, the joys and sorrows of my life and its most intimate moments are all recorded in two shelves of journals stretching back over all the years since I met Jesus. The other day I told my son they would make really interesting reading for him and our other children one day: but not, I added hastily, before I turn up my toes!

How about you? Do you aspire to be the friend God has made you to be? There are people out there waiting for you to introduce them to him; if you don't get to them, someone or something else will. Fall in love with God through his word; get into the word and get the word into you. . .oh, and go and buy that journal!

7

A Church for All Nations

The destiny of being a global church

I remember receiving a card out of the blue from Jiang Hong many months after our return from France, and the surge of affection as I read her news. Jiang Hong first came to our attention when we prayed for her at the end of a service. As it is now, so it was our custom then to offer to pray for people after the service every week. As was often the case at Belleville, room to move was scarce as many flocked forward, so one met people rather up close and personal! Thus I came upon Jiang Hong with her tear-stained face. The Spirit of God was working in her and she came to confirm her desire to be fully committed to whatever path God would lead her in. Like so many, she was awake to and in pursuit of her destiny.

We came to know Jiang Hong well, and she opened the door to an exciting friendship with the Chinese church that met in our premises every Sunday afternoon, since she was the only language link between them and us. Despite her origins, she remained throughout our time in Paris, and does still to this day, a faithful member of the church for all nations, as we nicknamed the Eglise Reformée de Paris, Belleville. Like so many, she was and is an illustration of the nations flocking to the cities, and one of the things we loved so deeply about Belleville was the family of at least 35 nations that we represented together. By the time we left, there were a dozen mixed-race marriages, most of whom had presented the church with a child, thus creating an even more exotic colour scheme for this family that we were so proud to belong to. The church is a people and a body to which it is part of our destiny to belong, and the perfect forum for creating friendships. That it is our destiny as followers of Christ to mix with the nations is clear from the book of Revelation:

> After this I looked and there before me was a great multitude that no one could count, from every nation, tribe, people and language, standing before the throne and in front of the Lamb.[1]

The apostle John is describing his vision, given to him on the island of Patmos where he was exiled towards the end of his life. The vision came to him on the Lord's Day while he was in the Spirit. What does this mean? It means that he was in prayer and that he had connected with heaven. Like Stephen and Paul before him and like multitudes down the centuries after him, heaven was open to him and he was instructed to record his vision initially for seven churches in Asia Minor, and thus for posterity.[2]

The church is a unique body of people in many respects. It is, as someone has said, the only club that exists for the benefit of its non-members. It is the only forum on earth where bonds of love and friendship can successfully unite individuals who are diverse in every respect other than their common commitment to and love of Jesus Christ. It is the Holy Grail that the human spirit searches for in terms of proving the unparalleled nature of love as incarnated by Jesus. There is no other place on earth that exhibits so conclusively the fruit of reconciliation, so powerfully the nature of true brotherhood and true community.

History records hundreds of illustrations of this from the founding of the Early Church in the book of Acts to the birth of the Pentecostal Church at the dawn of the twentieth century. One of the most exhilarating examples of co-operation and mutual submission is the coming together of the Fijian church leaders in recognition of their need of one another in the wake of the 2000 uprising. Laying aside their differences, they came together in prayer and saw extraordinary answers: an abating of violence; their prime minister openly confessing his faith and reliance on God; and many coming to Christ.[3]

In contrast, what do we see as we look around the world? A never-ending sequence of tribal hostilities, often resulting in open conflict, if not outright war, is played out before us. Tribes are not necessarily familial or even national: they can be religious, political, ideological, elitist, sectarian or ethical.

Patrick Dixon, in his book *Futurewise*, throws out a challenge to be prepared for what the future will bring us in a world,

which is being transformed before our eyes from an emerging industrial revolution and a technological post-war society into something altogether new and different. This millennium will witness the greatest challenges to human survival in human history, and many of them will face us in the early years of its first century. It will also provide us with science and technology beyond our greatest imaginings, and the greatest shift in values for over fifty years.[4]

He identifies six faces of the future, one of which is tribalism. There have been countless negative expressions of tribalism, many within our lifetime: ethnic cleansing during the Second World War, in Bosnia, Kosovo, Rwanda and Uganda; in the opening years of the new millennium, we watched helplessly as the Janjaweed forces in the Darfur region of the Sudan ruthlessly committed genocide. Our sensibilities were further anaesthetised by the school massacre in September 2004 in the previously unknown small town of Beslan in Ossetia, itself an unknown province of Russia to the majority of westerners.

Territory is at the root of tribalism, demonstrating the profoundly acquisitive and egocentric nature of man. Unless we are individually rewired to be followers of the man who had nowhere to lay his head and no possessions,[5] and who uttered the counter-cultural statement: 'If anyone would come after me, he must deny himself and take up his cross daily and follow me. For whoever wants to save his life will lose it, but whoever loses his life for me will save it,[6] we will never escape the constraints of tribalism, for competition and conflict are rooted in the human psyche since the time of Cain and Abel.

Patrick argues, however, that tribalism is,

an immensely positive force. Tribalism is the basis of all family, team and belonging. Tribalism provides a sense of identity.

Tribalism helps us understand who we are, where we've come from and where we're headed. . .Without tribes there is no geography in our relationships because there are no groups, just atomised collections of isolated individuals relating equally to everyone. Therefore if you want to understand the forces on someone's life, their motivation, the basis of their values and decisions, you need first to understand the person's own tribal culture.[7]

John's revelation of heaven reveals people from every tribe. No matter what tribe we originate from, the tribal identification that will cause us to be what and who we were destined by God to be, is that one that marks us out as followers of Jesus Christ. It is then in the context of the other tribes to which we belong—the workplace, the multinational corporation, the ethnic group, the blood family and so on—that we can aspire to being the aroma of Christ through which the fragrance of knowledge of him can be spread.[8]

Living in a global village has meant that the nations have come to the cities and to the churches, and this in turn has created the opportunity to discover what God is doing in the nations at first hand, and also to see him sowing from nation to nation. At the same time, those with jobs that take them to the nations come back with stories of what they have seen. These stories raise faith and encourage people where they are flagging or weighed down by their personal and local cares and concerns.

In 1999 we travelled to Brazil to visit Shalom, the group of churches planted and developed over some 30 years by our friends Harry and Elaine Scates. We first met Harry in 1997 when he was on an expedition to Europe as a Brazilian missionary (though of American origin, the Scates had taken Brazilian nationality). He came with a Brazilian organisation called Go To The Nations!. Some hundred Brazilians, ranging from a teenage girl to a politician in his fifties, gathered in Manchester, the UK base of the mission. After a few days, they were divided into smaller groups and set off for a week or so in different European capitals, one of which was Paris. During the planning stages of all this, I had felt stirred to undertake the administration of the Parisian visitation, perhaps sensing an important cross-fertilisation to be imminent.

And so it was that I went to greet this collection of total strangers at the Gare du Nord. Each day of their visit we listened to tales of God's Spirit poured out in Brazil; tales of churches growing, of hundreds giving their lives to Christ, of children being filled with a spirit of prayer, testimonies of how individual lives were completely turned around and transformed from despair to hope. One of these was Jose Maria, a 'son in the Lord' to Harry, just as Timothy and Titus were to Paul, now living in Lyon with his wife Rosangela and their two little daughters, with the goal of planting a church in the tough soil of France.

In 1999, we were seeing for ourselves. Travelling up to Uberlandia in the heart of Brazil where Harry and Elaine live, we stopped for a night at the town of Ribera da Prata where we attended the Shalom Sunday evening service. I'll never forget it. The worship was exuberant, excited and high volume; there were costumed dancers who created an amazing visual show of movement and colour; but the high point for me was the moment when they called for a time of praying for the nations. In a crowd movement that would have greatly alarmed any average English churchgoer, we swept to the stage area, invited to pray for whatever nation we wanted to. Each nation was represented by its national flag, flags being a standard part of the equipment for these Brazilian churches.

We made straight for the French flag and began to pour out our hearts to the Lord for the nation he had called us to so clearly in 1992. I found myself weeping almost immediately, able to release lots of the pain I had accumulated through the inevitable highs and lows of life, framed for me by building church in a foreign country. The Brazilians are a noisy crowd—they have been described as the world's troubadours, and they are certainly dynamically creative in the realm of the arts—and with them I felt quite uninhibited in expressing my longings for the church in Belleville, in Paris, in France. But the real snapshot in my memory album was when they wrapped us in the huge flag, and *they* began to weep over us and for us.

The rest of our trip continued to unfold the riches of the Brazilian church. We were there to teach a marriage seminar, but I remain convinced that we learned far more than we taught. We drank in their amazing hospitality, as they often gathered after church for a long, late and uproarious evening meal in a restaurant; or took us to experience the unforgettable churrascaria restaurant at which an array of different meats were offered and then cooked on mobile grills around the table. We loved their wonderfully eventful services, with every generation seemingly happily integrated; we were moved by the passionate prayer uttered with tears by young children; and we were impressed by their work among the poor through the orphanage established and run by the church.

The list was endless and we returned invigorated to Paris, where we soon purchased a set of international flags, which were cleverly installed by Jean-Claude, our quixotic handyman (whose principal work was leading the youth department of Youth With A Mission) for whom no task suggested by Charlie was beyond his ability or inventiveness. He is a true illustration of the dictum that where there's a will there's a way! The church in all nations was making us a church for all nations.

Elsewhere I have described the uplifting experience of walking on Prayer Mountain near Kampala. The annual AfriCamp prayer conference, part of which takes place on Prayer Mountain, likewise inspires faith and energy, not solely through its culturally alien but exciting presentation. The contributors may speak more loudly than we are used to, but they speak with authority and grace, releasing courage in the listener. With the typical reservation of the British, I may have been alarmed or exhausted by the experience of praying at such a volume that I couldn't hear myself, let alone the others in my group; or repulsed by the body odours of those pressed up against me in the crowd; but I have yet to come across anyone who has not caught fire from a visit to AfriCamp and seen dramatic changes in their prayer life.

One of my most colourful memories is of a celebration following a marriage conference we had taught in the north of Togo. As dawn stole across the sky, and we heard the familiar creaking of the well as it was cranked into action outside our window, we heard the bleating of the goat as it was led protesting to the slaughter and knew we were hearing the last cries of our lunch! Hours later the celebration

was under way and began with a renewal of vows cere-
mony for the participating couples. How moving it was to
watch the primary-educated men with their mostly illiterate wives share a common covenant with us from whom
they were so different. Next Joseph, who with his wife
oversaw the Community Health Programme, took the stage
in order to hand out 20 condoms to each couple, emphasis-
ing cheerfully that they were for single use. All this to the
accompaniment of riotous laughter and cheering. Catching
one another's eyes, Charlie and I mutually acknowledged a
glorious kingdom moment, before sitting down to consume
the goat stew, cooked to a turn by the female kitchen crew
in a corner of the compound.

Towards the end of our time in Paris, the relationship
with the Chinese Church that had begun with the arrival of
Jiang Hong had developed to the point of a visit to their
home provinces being earnestly requested by the leaders of
the church. The church was affiliated to a denomination
with churches in many parts of the world, but principally in
China and in Hong Kong where the headquarters are situ-
ated. So a trip was arranged, and Jiang Hong, Jean-Claude
and Benedicte, the much-loved church secretary who had
been involved with Open Doors for many years, set off.
Back they came, armed with photos and stories, and poured
inspiration and faith into the family at home. As a church
family we were affected and inspired by different aspects of
the global church of Jesus in each country: the faith and
development of the Togolese church, initiated by the outworking of the fourfold vision of the ministry of Jesus, to
plant churches, dig wells, build schools and inaugurate co-
operatives; the extraordinary corporate prayer life of the

Ugandans, called forth out of them by the desperate plight of their nation under the successive dictatorships of Amin and Obote in the 80s; the courage and bravery of the Chinese who gathered in remote areas to learn about God and be equipped to lead churches under persecution.

More recently, we have been privileged to meet and listen to Brother Yun, nicknamed The Heavenly Man, the title of the book that describes his pilgrimage through persecution and torture following his conversion to Christ.[9] The name Heavenly Man stemmed from an incident in 1984 when Brother Yun refused to reveal his real name to the authorities knowing it would compromise and endanger his fellow Christians. In response to threats and beatings from the Public Security Bureau to disclose his name and address, he shouted, 'I am a heavenly man! My home is in heaven!' Hearing this, his friends, the local believers were able to flee and escape arrest.

Yun was captivating; he seemed to overflow with love, and I found myself struggling to comprehend the ability to undergo so much suffering and yet be so full of praise for God. In no way do I have any tribal affinity with such a godly man; with the crucial exception of our common faith in Jesus, his so much stronger than mine, and seemingly etched in the lines of his compelling face. One of God's purposes in calling us to belong to the international church is of course to challenge us where we are lazy or apathetic, indisciplined or self-centred. Men and women from around the world who have followed Jesus' injunction to take up their cross and lose their lives will confront us with areas of our lives where we are indulging ourselves or compromising our faith; they will bring sharply into focus what God is really doing in and with his church and they will stimulate and goad us to return to our first love, to repent and to do the things we did at first.[10]

It is your destiny and mine to belong to the church for all nations and the church in all nations. To continually broaden our comprehension of how God is inexorably fulfilling his plans and purposes throughout the earth, it behoves us to keep our finger on the pulse of the world-wide church: not just so that we know what is really happening (information we will never come by through the newspaper or the television), but so that our perspective is correct and healthy; so that we can see the incomparable riches of his grace because we are seated with God in the heavenly realms thanks to Jesus.

> There is nothing like the local church when it's working right. Its beauty is indescribable. Its power is breathtaking. Its potential is unlimited. It comforts the grieving and heals the broken in the context of community. It builds bridges to seekers and offers truth to the confused. It provides resources for those in need and opens its arms to the forgotten, the downtrodden, the disillusioned. It breaks the chains of addictions, frees the oppressed, and offers belonging to the marginalized of this world. Whatever the capacity for human suffering, the church has a greater capacity for healing and wholeness.
>
> Still to this day, the potential of the local church is almost more than I can grasp. No other organization on earth is like the church. Nothing even comes close.[11]

8

All You Need Is Love

The greatest destiny

As a child I used to dream that one day I would hold audiences captive by playing a piano while dancing on the keys and singing as I played and danced! I think this vision may have been triggered by seeing Picasso's 'Circus Acrobat'. I longed with all my being to be a performer, an artist with gifts that merited being displayed. By the time I was wading in the shallows of adulthood, I knew this vision was eluding me, and somewhere in the recesses of my subconscious I knew that it would always elude me. Reality was never going to meet the fantasy. At the same time, life's path had thrown me among artists of every description. My boyfriend's family and many of their entourage were wonderfully bohemian, many of them actors and artists, and he himself was a talented actor, albeit amateur. Oxford days were spent in a dizzy whirl among writers and poets, actors and producers. I was hungry to learn and yearned to be on a par with any one of them. I threw myself into any opportunity that presented itself.

Then I split up with the boyfriend, moved to another city and encountered God (a story I come to at the end of the book). Once again I found myself in an artistic milieu, invited to participate in open-air sketches on a beach mission. Once again my appetite was whetted, my ambitions were fanned into flame and my hopes rose.

But one day, alone in my room, I confronted my limitations. By now, daily dialogue with my heavenly Father was the norm and I poured out my heart and my tears as I acknowledged that no one was ever going to exclaim about my talent or write about my amazing gifts! I suppose it's amusing, but it was painful as I struggled to come to terms with the fate of being born without the aptitudes I so longed to have. I wrote a long letter about all of this, pouring out my sense of inadequacy and my feelings of insecurity to someone who had become a close friend during my months of searching to make sense of God, and who had answered many of my questions about faith, Jesus and the Christian hope. Soon afterwards he wrote back; a twelve-page letter that I still have, for it contained such wisdom, encouragement and consolation, and in itself made a significant contribution to my being able to press on and escape from the binding feelings of hopelessness and failure.

This is some of what he said:

This is what God says to those caught on that particular fork: 'I will bend it into my cross and you shall carry it and learn from me. You will be weighed in the scales of the world and found wanting, but your achievement will last when all this world and its scales have vanished into oblivion, for your work will be the work of love. You will not work with the shape of things that perish, but with the shape of people, destined for eternity. My greatest achievement is not the making of this world, though all men, including many who do not obey me, praise me for this; my greatest achievement is in the shaping of your soul. Work then with me to shape the souls of others, and from this very day your achievement will be recorded in the book of life.'

Famously above everything else, Paul says,

If I speak in the tongues of men and of angels, but have not love, I am only a resounding gong or a clanging cymbal. If I have the gift of prophecy and can fathom all mysteries and all knowledge, and if I have a faith that can move mountains, but have not love, I am nothing. If I give all I possess to the poor, and surrender my body to the flames, but have not love, I gain nothing.[1]

John says that the proof of loving God is that we love each other: indeed he emphasises that to be in any way deficient in love towards our fellow man annuls any claim we might make to be a lover of God, because God is love. And Jesus said that it's by the love we show one another that all men would know that we are his disciples. I once challenged a fellow teacher with this truth, because each day in the staffroom she would give vent to her resentment and criticism of other members of staff who were not present. My audacity unleashed a torrent of anger, and I shudder to think what came over me. No doubt she thought I was a little upstart; and I was. I was in my probationary year of teaching and, although filled with the fire of the newly converted (and no doubt a good dose of self-righteousness), my cause was not helped by the fact that I still smoked and used to cadge a cigarette off this very woman most days, having stopped buying them as a strategy for giving up!

It is not our doctrine that will draw men to God, nor our

style of worship, nor even our response to the poor. Behind all these lies a key without which they are but a resounding gong or a clanging cymbal.

Men, women and children are thirsty for love because they are created to give and receive love. 'The hunger for love is much more difficult to remove than the hunger for bread,' said Mother Teresa, who was perhaps uniquely qualified to make such a statement. She also said that the success of loving lies not in its fruit but in the loving itself.

Of course a person may be a loving artist of one kind or another; this is no longer a dilemma to me, for I am content to be a lover of souls alone. However, multitudes of artists have trodden a tortured path where love and its expression are concerned. The success so often achieved by the gifted is equally often the very thing that frustrates their search for love. Boris Becker, the famous tennis star of the 90s, said, 'I had everything, from flights on Concorde to the best hotels. Everything but love. And I was very lonely.'

In the universal quest for love, artists take their place alongside every workman in every sphere of life, be he plumber, policeman or physician. Where then is love to be found? First of all I think it is found in the disposition of a man or woman who has discovered something of the real presence of God; not God as a benefactor, but God as a Father, God as perfect lover of their soul. Such were many of the mystics, who lingered over their communion with God. Therese de Lisieux, Henri Nouwen, Julian of Norwich, St John of the Cross all knew about this.

I was at the most dangerous time of life for young girls, but God did for me what Ezekiel recounts:[2] Passing by me, Jesus saw that I was ripe for love. He plighted his troth to me and I became his. He threw his cloak about me, washed me with water and anointed me with oil, clothed me with fine linen and silk and decked me with bracelets and priceless gems. He fed me on wheat and honey and oil and I had matchless beauty and He made me a queen. Jesus did all that for me. Jesus did all that for me.[3]

Something so intimate could never be born of head knowledge. Lest we should think this to be an exclusively female response to God, listen to Brother Lawrence, the seventeenth century monastery chef:

The King, full of mercy and goodness, very far from chastising me, embraces me with love, makes me eat at his table, serves me with His own hands, gives me the key of His treasures. He converses and delights Himself with me incessantly. . .

And to Jim Elliot, the missionary martyr of the 1950s:

Oh the fullness, pleasure, sheer excitement of knowing God on Earth! I care not if I never raise my voice again for him, if only I may love Him, please Him. Maybe in His mercy he shall give me a host of children that I may lead them through the vast star fields to explore his delicacies whose finger ends set them to burning. But if not, if only I may see Him, touch his garments, smile into His eyes—ah then, not stars nor children shall matter, only Himself.[4]

Count Ludwig van Zinzendorf, born in 1700, has been called by historians the rich young ruler who said yes. He was born into one of the great families in Europe and destined for the Emperor's Court, but he gave it all up and instead spent his great fortune on carrying the gospel to the ends of the earth through the Moravian Church for whom he was a leader and provider.[5] Why? Because he met the risen Christ:

> While completing his tour of the great European cities, Zinzendorf visited an art museum in Dusseldorf. There he happened upon Domencio Feti's Ecce Homo, Behold the Man, a striking portrait of Jesus crowned with thorns. The inscription read, 'I have done this for you. What have you done for me?' The Count was stunned. 'I have loved him for so long,' mused the young nobleman, 'but I have not really done anything for him.' Standing before the portrait, Zinzendorf made a commitment that would become the compelling focus for the rest of his life. 'From now on I will do whatever he leads me to do,' he vowed. He stayed true to this commitment for the rest of his life. . .[6]

He taught unity and lived it, loving and befriending Lutherans, Moravians, Pietists, Puritans, Anabaptists and Catholics; and would never judge a man by his doctrinal or denominational affiliation, but by the content of his heart.

Such individuals have a magnetic attraction that draws one as a lamp draws a moth. While a moth is often literally consumed in the flame, we will find the sharp edges of our characters imperceptibly honed in the company of such saints, for there is something of the presence of God that compels us at once to seek them out and subdue our passions. All such people have yielded to the hunger for God that is written into the human soul, but that for many is suppressed or suffocated. They have sought intimacy with God and paid a price for it. Knowledge of God has been chosen over knowledge of the world or by the world. Like Thomas à Kempis, and like Paul, they have understood that the highest of ambitions is to live in the imitation of Christ.

Today there is a recovery of the yearning for God's presence and company as it is expressed in Psalm 63: 'O God, you are my God, earnestly I seek you; my soul thirsts for you, my body longs for you, in a dry and weary land where there is no water.'[7]

It is this yearning that is at the root of the outbreaks of what is known as the Father's love in places as far apart as Toronto in Canada and Macon in France. In these places and others, normal religious procedure and ritual have been taken over by an outpouring of response to God; breaking out of all the accepted forms of corporate religious practice, liturgical and less liturgical. As with all revivals, the tares have grown with the wheat, feathers have been ruffled and the guardians of doctrine have snatched up their concordances and their commentaries. Many foolish controversies have arisen and many have been distracted by foolish and stupid arguments. What is this all about? It is about an impatience with the restrictions of religion as opposed to the freedom of relationship, and about a passion for righteousness as found in the intimate company of God himself.

I remember years ago visiting St Aldate's long before we ever dreamt of coming to work there, and hearing Michael Green preach a passionate gospel message. The church was excitingly crowded, and in the middle of his sermon a young man shouted out a challenge: How do you know that leading someone to Christ is the greatest of all experiences, it can't be better than sex? (For Michael had indeed had the temerity to make such a claim, typically daring and dangerous!) There was an electric silence as the assembled company waited to see how Michael would extricate himself. And this he did, with boldness and confidence; for those who know God are completely unthreatened by challenges that spring from cultural norms, but know nothing of sweet communion with Jesus.

But the point of this cameo is that the shout of the young man, appearing at first like a witty challenge that turned the atmosphere from one of studious attentiveness to one of theatrical tension, was really a heart cry. For so many the yearning for intimacy and tenderness, expressed through sexual experience, has not been met. The inner void remains, growing more painful with every disappointment, but so does the heart cry; and the call to those of us who have found mercy and met Jesus is to be a conduit of him to the multitudes who are like that young man. Many are finding the way to be a conduit through these so-called and contentious wells of revival in places like Toronto.

As with Mother Teresa, a love affair with God must necessarily issue forth in works of love, for all that we receive we want only to give away. And to fall in love with God will lead us to turn our western value system upside down and be drawn to the poor.

Heidi and Rolland Baker[8] are unusual missionaries: they have degrees in systematic theology and work in Mozambique with illiterate pastors who raise people from the dead but don't speak in tongues! Heidi is also an unusual conference speaker; one who flops over the lectern and delivers her talk supine beneath it, overwhelmed by the presence of God. If all our checking systems slam into place as we read of this curiosity, how much more will we question if we see it: I know, because I have. Yet in fact we are displaying nothing other than the reaction of the Pharisees every time Jesus showed his power, either through healing or through breaking religious laws or tradition. Real love is at once threatening and overwhelming, but it is what we are called to if we are going to live a life of destiny, and it will earn us foes as well as friends, criticism as well as praise. Why are we so surprised? After all, Jesus said,

> . . .count yourselves blessed every time people put you down or throw you out or speak lies about you to discredit me. What it means is that the truth is too close for comfort and they are uncomfortable. You can be glad when that happens—give a cheer, even!—for though they don't like it, *I* do! And all heaven applauds. And know that you are in good company. My prophets and witnesses have always gotten into this kind of trouble.[9]

All of this is a fearful challenge to the mindset and outlook into which we are born and in which we grow up in the western world. We are taught to acquire, and to collect, to take and to multiply, whether the object be education, possessions, money or knowledge. One of the most magnetic truths about Jesus is his reversal of all this. If you want to come with me, he says, you'll be on the road, or lodging with my friends, for I own no home.[10] How do you get eternal life? He continues. Well, you need to sell all your possessions and give the proceeds to the poor, then your wealth will be in heaven.[11] Knowledge, said Paul, puffs up, but love builds up.[12] This from a man who had an impeccable pedigree as far as the Jewish authorities were concerned.[13] But he had discovered something that went beyond the normal heights of achievement. He had been caught up to paradise, and heard inexpressible things that a man is not permitted to tell[14]—in the sense that he cannot tell, because no human language is adequate to tell such things—and it had changed his life. It had made him ready to bear anything in order to communicate Christ and see the yearnings of people like that young man in St Aldate's met.

Paul endured beatings, imprisonment, riots, hard work, sleepless nights and hunger. He endured dishonour, bad report, being considered a fraud and misunderstanding.[15] Why? Why would a man who had so much to gain be prepared to stake his reputation on preaching Jesus Christ? How could a man of his stature, humanly speaking, write to the Philippian church that he would prefer to die and be with Christ,[16] and that if he did it would be much better than being in prison, as he currently is. He is there, not for any crime other than having had the audacity to be very outspoken about Jesus in front of the Roman authorities. The attraction of being dead rather than imprisoned certainly wasn't because conditions in the prison were unbearable. The end of the book of Acts tells us he was allowed to live by himself with a soldier to guard him, and that the leaders of the Jews came in large numbers to a pre-arranged meeting with him in that place.[17] No. Paul had seen heaven open and it had changed the course of his life; he now lived only to talk about Jesus and be an agent of his power; and Paul's presence and exhortations in the canon of scripture are a call to us to be imitators of him. In a sense we all need a Damascus road experience because capturing the heart of Jesus is a matter of revelation not reason, as the stories of Nicodemus, Gamaliel, Paul and Peter, to name but a few, bear ample testimony.

I often feel frustrated and captive to a western expression of church. Sometimes I tell people how I would love to have trained as a nurse instead of a teacher and be equipped to leave houses, brothers, sisters, father, mother, children and fields for his sake, and to go and lose myself where there are few possessions, little shelter, much sickness and a deficit of love.

My father took a decision with my mother, when I was about 15, to go and serve a school in Uganda, where we then spent our holidays for the years they lived there. Although the majority of our time was spent in the company of the expatriate community, a love for the place and the people somehow lodged in my being and fed into me the conviction that I was called to love all people equally. Many years later, I would come to understand those years as part of God's design for my life and destiny.

The first real opportunity I had to exercise this conviction was during our years in Paris, living in the cosmopolitan 19th arrondissement, seething with humanity from all the corners of the globe: walking down the Rue de Belleville, the main arterial road leading to the centre of the city, was like taking a stroll through the nations. People originating from China, Cambodia, Vietnam, Afghanistan, the Ivory Coast, Burkina Faso, Congo, Mali, Togo, Benin, Algeria, Morocco and Tunisia mingled with members of the significant Jewish community (after the United States, Paris boasts the largest Jewish community outside Israel), and the numerous West Indians who come to Paris from the francophone islands that form part of the French colonies. Europe was there too, Polish and Russian alongside Portuguese and British. Even the Americans came to Belleville!

And the poor walked the streets, and begged as they do in every city of every nation. Marina lived in the old and dilapidated block of flats next to our ugly 1960s block. Behind the crumbling façade of No. 1 lay a rather beautiful if unkempt garden, where its inhabitants hung their washing and enjoyed communal barbecues in the summer months. Here Marina often roamed, shrieking in her deep and hoarse voice.

I began by approaching her in the street, only to be rebuffed as she turned away. It was my first lesson in understanding that the poor are seldom grateful for one's interventions. But I persisted through the years, inviting her into my kitchen for a coffee one day, taking clothes to her (which she declined since she was shortly going to collect her own from another planet!), visiting the dingy, dirty and chaotic apartment that she shared with her sister and teenage niece, and engaging in what approximated to a conversation as often as I could. Marina's mind had long been shot by a combination of abuse, traumatic experiences and electro-therapy for a period when she had consented to psychiatric treatment. Loving the poor is really hard. You can't do it with a return in mind. We can't do it with building our church in mind. At least not in the way we are tempted to interpret what that means. I think though that every loving approach to the broken, whatever the outcome or fruit, may be counted in heaven as building the church, despite us not seeing another bottom on another seat on Sunday.

In Belleville it was impossible to shut your eyes to the poor. They lay beneath our windows at night; they knocked at our door with amazing stories of just needing a hundred francs to feed their little children until their money came through; they roamed the streets, challenging our lifestyle by their very presence; they came into our church with their dogs and their incontinence and their overpowering odours; and they daily threw down the challenge: Do you know what love means? They taught us that love is not an equation. I love, therefore I am loved. No. I love, therefore I am reviled and ridiculed; I am taken for a ride. The poor can be very wily as well as winsome.

One Sunday, when Charlie was away, I was called to the back of the church to talk to a young man who said he longed to find God again and change the existence life had dealt him through circumstance and foolish decisions. He had decided to come to the church regularly, and had dug out his Bible from among his possessions. However, first he needed to go to Grenoble to his dying mother, so could we help him with the fare? Together with one of the elders we talked for some time, seeking to discern whether this was genuine or not. He repeatedly and earnestly promised he would repay the loan. Finally persuaded, I accompanied him up the road to the cash point outside our bank and withdrew the 300 francs needed. It was as I put the money into his hand that I realised in an instant that I would never see either him or it again and began to berate myself internally for my stupidity. The poor can be brilliant thespians.

Opposite our house in Oxford, a world away from the noise and confusion of Belleville, is a fitness centre, and opposite our kitchen window, some two metres away, is the outlet of the extraction fan that heats and air conditions the centre. Here the homeless gather in winter to keep warm during the periods when they cannot access their hostels or shelters due to cleaning schedules. God, it seems, did not consider our move a reason to become immune to the call to love the poor! We live in the ongoing discomfort of that challenge.

To love the poor is not the extent of our mandate. We are called to love the rich, the arrogant, the hard-hearted, the powerful and the intellectual. We're called to pour out of ourselves a continuous overflow of God's love. So it stands to reason that only those who have an inflow of that same love could possibly pour it out. If an individual can be full of love, so can a church. What is the church but the assembly of all those who have had the amazing privilege of finding Jesus and submitting their lives to him, nailing their colours to the mast and determining to be his disciple? Where those who are called to lead—in other words to serve—the church have understood this upside down nature of love, you will find expressions of community that take your breath away; not only because there is a captivating beauty about the gathered people but because there is a perfume arising from them. The first time we encountered this was shortly after discovering Jesus, during a spell at St Michael-le-Belfry in York, under the leadership of David Watson, one of the giants of the evangelical church in the heyday of renewal. For the first time we saw colour, movement, noise, tears, laughter, healing, faith, energy, dancing, vision, preaching, worship and prayer all bound up and expressed in the life of a community drawn from all walks of life and from every generation.

The second time was in very different circumstances. We were washing around in the aftermath of the emotional vortex that caught us like a tornado after the death of Samuel. Every day there was a knock at the door, which revealed upon opening it a pie or a casserole or a dish in the lovingly extended arms of someone belonging to the church of which we were temporarily members for our three months in California. Another lesson: you don't have to know everyone in the church for the whole thing to work and be a source of love. They brought us more than pies in those weeks.

We may talk a great deal about destiny, and get distracted into believing it has to do with a career or a job; these things are important, but they are the vehicle of our destiny rather than the destiny itself, for we all share a common destiny. Many years ago, my father-in-law gave us a picture he had made. It is a simple phrase immortalised by Augustine, framed and beautifully decorated: *ama et fac quod vis*. 'Love and do as you please'. For Augustine it was understood that to love means to love God, for if we don't, we cannot truly love. In discovering the work or the career or even the calling for which we were born, we must fill it with loving God and loving each other, for these are the two great commandments that embrace all others.

So I say to you wherever you find yourself today as you consider the question of destiny: *ama et fac quod vis*!

9

Making Poverty History

The destiny of being a reformer

Injustice anywhere is a threat to justice everywhere.
(Martin Luther King)

One of the best loved chapters in the Bible is Isaiah 58. It is loved in spite of, or perhaps because of, the fact that it is a goad to the church. 'My people seem keen to know my ways, and seek me out as if they were those who understood how to act righteously, and hadn't turned their backs on my commands,' says God, through the lips of Isaiah; lips which, we might remember, have been touched with a live coal from the altar of the Temple which Isaiah saw in a vision when he heard the call to serve God as a prophet. So we know that his words are reliable.

So often when our motives or behaviour are questioned we defensively assume that the questioner is missing some information or hasn't understood. Here the Israelites are offended because after all they are fulfilling all the religious requirements, even fasting. And goodness knows that fasting is demanding enough and a sure proof of our godliness!

No; apparently not. Apparently, we need to loose the chains of injustice, set the oppressed free, release people from the shackles that restrict their movement, share our food with the hungry, give shelter to the homeless, provide clothes for those who are in rags, look after our own family, make righteous laws that are fair, and do away with gossip and backbiting. Oh, and we should observe the Sabbath and make provision for rest and worship in our schedule. Then and then only will we find answers to the questions we are asking God, for then much of the puzzle will be unscrambled; much that confounds us will suddenly make sense.

There have always been men and women who have spent themselves fighting for justice and equality. A universally well-known example is William Wilberforce who devoted himself to abolishing slavery in the nineteenth century. Yet we know that the passing of a law, though it may bring brief respite, cannot eradicate deceit and greed from the heart of man, nor his lust for power. Today there are more victims of slavery than in all the years prior to Wilberforce's Emancipation Bill of 1833: those who work in the sweatshops for the insatiable demands of the fashion industry; those who are captured to swell fighting armies and those who are trafficked for prostitution. The majority of these are women and children.

In Paris I would often take the Metro at our local station, Pyrenees, and get off three stops up at Telegraphe to visit my friend Christine Thabot at the church she and her husband, David, began some ten years ago. The innards of any city are both surprisingly beautiful and dirty, dark and dangerous; places that conceal poverty, pain and despair. In eastern Paris, doors could open to reveal breathtakingly beautiful gardens, festooned with stately trees, exotic plants and dazzling flowers, but they could also reveal misery. Walking up the alley that leads to the Thabots' church, I passed some large rooms. The windows of one of these were blacked out and through the small gap afforded by the door often being left ajar, presumably for air, I could see the curious combination of materials in every colour of the rainbow exotically draping the space, and the drab little figures that punctuated the colour as they hunched over their sewing machines. There were other sweatshops nearer our home, just yards from the Belleville church.

Slavery has many guises. Young girls seeking adventure and travel become au pair girls, expecting an agreeable if hardworking experience. But many find themselves working far more hours than they should and living on pay that is a pittance. Incomparably worse is the flourishing trade of trafficking children for prostitution. I wonder if you have become so used to this fact that it no longer sends shock waves through you when you read and hear about it. Examples abound. In January 2005 the national news carried the story of a 16-year-old from Lithuania who entrusted herself to an organisation that promised a job and freedom in the UK. Instead she found herself working in a brothel in Hounslow. Once she was no longer contactable, her mobile phone having run out of money, her family's suspicions were aroused and they contacted the British police, who tracked her down and organised her return home. She was a lucky one. Or was she? What sort of scars will be left after even a short period of serving men with her body? Older men, whose dreams have faded or been broken and who carry unbearable sorrow or revenge in their souls, are often those who buy sex. How easily will her scars tear open? Will she ever be able to trust a man enough to set up a permanent partnership with him? So often one abuse leads to another and the wounded seek healing where it cannot be found.

Another form of slavery is manifested where there is war. Far beyond the frontiers of Europe, boys as young as ten or twelve have been regularly kidnapped by the Janjaweed soldiers in the Darfur area of the Sudan or by the Lord's Resistance Army in the north of Uganda. In both cases these children are taken as troops to boost the numbers of fighting forces; in both cases they are made to fight their own people. The collective western conscience is vaguely disturbed by this, but not enough to ensure that such a practice ceases. After all, it's a long way away.

In 2003 we met the Bishop of Kitgum in northern Uganda, close to the area where the LRA operates. A couple of months later, Margaret, his wife, wrote to me:

> Two weeks ago, over ten people were killed in a camp near my village and about a month ago over 190 people were killed in Lira. Just about a week ago the government crossed into Sudan to attempt another Iron Fist operation to try and get the LRA out of Sudan. They have managed to get them out and into Uganda, Acholi land of which Kitgum is inclusive [sic]. Normally when the rebels cross like this the atrocity they do is terrible. . .people are without hope because they are imagining that if the few rebels who remained. . .can do mass killings like they did in Lira. . .what will happen when they are many? Sister, the situation needs nothing but prayers.

Several months later the Bishop himself was taken prisoner, but released unharmed. He and Margaret have chosen to stay with their people despite the danger, but have sent their children to school in Kampala. They are a couple who know the meaning both of destiny and of sacrifice. And many of those who cause them to live this knife-edge are themselves prisoners to those who have forced them to fight.

Slavery breeds poverty, and much of Margaret's letter was outlining simple projects which could alleviate the bleak conditions endured throughout their area.

> We have 44 pastors in the diocese. . .they are really in great need. They are living with the displaced people in camps without salaries because the people are in abject poverty and cannot manage to pay them. They come to beg for money from us who do not even have anything to offer them.

She was asking for financial aid to buy five grinding machines, one for each region so that maize distributed by the World Food Programme could be ground and sold and create a little income for food and schooling.

Perhaps our reaction is to think that giving money just plasters over the cracks; and indeed to some extent that is true. But can you just for a moment imagine a life without Tesco's; a life devoid of the material glut in which we live; a life without any form of credit spending? It is impossible for us to envisage really running out of bread.

For anyone to whom destiny is important, it must include loosing the chains of injustice, untying the cords of the yoke and setting free the oppressed. It must include sharing our food with the hungry and providing the poor wanderer with shelter. It must include clothing the naked and spending ourselves on behalf of the hungry.[1]

Many are those who have risen to this challenge; let's

look back at some of them, and at some who are contemporary.

Wilberforce became the leader of the abolition movement under Pitt the Younger in 1787. Two years later he made a speech that the newspapers praised as being one of the most eloquent ever to have been heard in the House. One reported that, 'The gallery of the House of Commons was crowded with Liverpool Merchants; who hung their heads in sorrow—for the African occupation of bolts and chains is no more.' But it was a premature announcement, for not until 1807 did Parliament vote overwhelmingly in favour of abolition, and even then slavery remained a reality in the British colonies. Another 26 years were to pass before this too was abolished through the Emancipation Bill of 1833; three days later, Wilberforce died, having truly laid down his life for his brothers and done what he was created to do.

Josephine Butler was another nineteenth-century reformer whose heart propelled her into destiny.

> Josephine was encouraged by her father, not only to think for herself, but also to believe it was her Christian duty to improve the lot of the people in her orbit. She couldn't help but contrast her own comfortable, protected life with the appalling poverty and deprivation to be found elsewhere. . . At one point it filled her with doubts about the existence of a loving God. How could there be such huge inequalities? Why did God allow his creatures to suffer or tolerate such blatant abuses of power? Why was his church so uncaring and ineffectual?[2]

Josephine went on to fight for 20 years for the repeal of the Contagious Disease Acts of the 1860s. These gave the police the power to subject any lone woman suspected of prostitution to a brutal internal examination to check for signs of venereal disease. The physical consequences of this were multiple, including miscarriage or permanent internal damage causing sterility, not to mention the emotional effects. Meeting destitute girls in a Liverpool workhouse, whose only source of income was prostitution, convinced her that they were not wicked and licentious, but the victims of circumstance and of predatory men.

Josephine Butler became a great and courageous crusader on behalf of such women, openly challenging the responsibility of men towards them and sacrificing much time with her family; but she was also beautiful, and had to endure much heckling, crude abuse and innuendo when she spoke in public. Her husband George had released and encouraged her in her calling, yet they had to endure rumours of a failing marriage and obscene drawings of her sent through the post. They also had to bear long separations as she travelled the country to make known her cause. Not until 1833 did she hear the reading of a bill to repeal discriminatory Acts, from the Ladies Gallery of the House of Commons, at 1.30am.

Deeply moved, she went out onto the terrace overlooking the Thames.

> The fog had cleared away and it was very calm under the starlit sky. All the bustle of the city was stilled and the only sound was that of the dark water lapping against the buttresses of the broad stone terrace. . .it almost seemed like a dream.[3]

One of the most remarkable things about Josephine Butler was that all this took place following the tragic death of her little girl Eva, an adored daughter born to her and George after three sons. The accident took place at home when the child, rushing to greet them on their return, fell through the collapsing banisters to her death. Her story is magnificently inspiring for any who have been stopped in their tracks by tragedy, and a call to rise up and walk on.[4]

Many of my own forebears were Quakers, and of particular note are James and Mary Ellis who retired in 1848 from a successful worsted manufacturing business in Bradford to move to Letterfrack in Connemara. They were deeply distressed by reports of the famine in Ireland, and the relief work they set up was an individual response to try to alleviate the terrible poverty and starvation caused during the famine. The many letters written by Mary reveal the frightening deprivation of this time; she describes the conditions they found on a visit soon after their arrival. The cabin they entered was,

> . . .about nine feet by six, with no furniture. . .but a little stool, about six inches high. . .so down we sat against the wall, and close to our feet, two of the gentlest little bairns, about three and four years old, with their feet almost in a little bit of the fire.[5]

She describes their meal of cockles and then the family's story of misfortune:

> . . .six years ago they had two cows and were doing well, when the famine came; one cow went after another, the last for £2.10. Then her husband fell ill and never since have they had food enough to eat. But the semi-nudity! The three poor little creatures had each a strip of woollen rag stitched upon them, but all in strips, not covering either a limb or any side of their

body, yet they were all children one could love well. . .They
had lessened their cabin this last week to sell two sticks for six-
pence. There are two little skeletons in another cabin, I think
too far gone to be restored.[6]

The Ellises lived in Letterfrack from 1849 to 1857, and
accomplished much that has long outlived them. Having
built a family home, James began by employing 80 men to
drain the bogland, plant thousands of trees and construct
walls, gardens and roads. Next came a school/meeting
house, dispensary, shop and temperance hall, along with
cottages for his employees. Mary visited the poor, distributing money to urgent cases of distress from a private fund.

Today Letterfrack is a thriving community and, 150 years
later, the schoolhouse still stands as a legacy of the Ellises'
commitment to it. Connemara West is a college linked with
Galway University where students train in practical crafts
such as furniture-making, and behind the imposing build-
ings one enters the National Connemara Park and its Visitor
Centre which tells the Ellis story. On holiday with my parents in 2004, we met the principal and were given a tour of
the college. What a testimony to the lasting fruit borne by
people who grasped hold of their destiny through allowing
compassion to give birth to action!

Like history, the pages of the Bible are liberally scattered
with such noble people. One to whom I am specially drawn
is Esther, a humble girl who was plucked from obscurity to
become one of the greatest of Jewish heroines. Unlike
many, her family had remained in Persia after most Jews
had returned from their exile to Jerusalem. An orphan, we
first meet her cooped up in a harem of young virgins from

among whom the capricious king will choose a queen to replace Vashti, rejected for failing to obey his every whim. Esther is judged pleasing to the king and begins a life as queen. Some years later, her uncle, who has brought her up *in loco parentis*, reveals to Esther his discovery of a plot to exterminate all Jews; a plot instigated by the most senior politician in the land, Haman. A crisis of this magnitude demands a response, and Mordecai asks Esther to appeal to the king. Approaching the king without being summoned risked the death penalty, but Mordecai was firm. 'Don't think you're special enough to be spared if our people are destroyed,' he tells her. 'In any case if you don't intervene on our behalf, someone will. . .'[7]

What a moment of choice for this young girl, until now a submissive and acquiescent character who had always sought to please, whether Mordecai, Hegai the chief eunuch, or the king himself! She could so easily have declined the request, fearing for her life. But instead, a new Esther seems to rise up; an Esther ready to risk everything; position, status, reputation, and even her life. She asks Mordecai to call a fast and participates in it with her maids. At the end of the three days she is received by the king, despite the contravention of protocol, and the story of the salvation of the Jews unfolds steadily from that moment on.

All these people have a selflessness in common; they are ready to give everything up for the sake of justice and righteousness. 'If there is a right place for us, I think my chief desire is that we may be in it, even if it be in exile.'[8]

Nor do they seek fame; '. . .we have no inclination to be published. As long as we live in the remembrance of our friends, and under the protecting care and approbation of the Best of Friends, we do not care how obscurely we pass on. . .'[9] They are not so much asking: What is your will for my individual life, with its inevitable subtext of wanting to be special; but more: What is your will and what is my part in it? Of course, each individual is uniquely hand-crafted, and so to be special is a given. The question is how we will seek to employ whatever makes us special in favour of others; that is to truly live out our destiny.

Many are the saints and heroes who have done what they were created to do. Some, like Wilberforce and Josephine Butler, are known, but many, like the Ellises, are mostly unsung. We can conjure many names to mind: The Earl of Shaftesbury, perhaps the best-loved benefactor and politician of the nineteenth century, whose tireless compassionate work on behalf of the poor and oppressed earned him the affectionate title of 'The Poor Man's Earl'; Florence Nightingale; Bishop Hannington; David Livingstone; the roll-call is long. In our own times, the procession has continued. Martyrs, politicians and ordinary people, made extraordinary by their response to a call from deep within, make up this royal procession that makes its stately way through the pages of our history.

Interestingly, all these men and women had a deep faith in God; of James Ellis it was written: '. . .his life showed that Christianity was, with him, a living principle, and we believe it may be truly said that "he feared God and hated covetousness".'[10] During Wilberforce's early years in Parliament, 'he did not involve himself at first with any great cause. A sudden conversion to evangelical Christianity in 1785 changed that and from then onwards he approached politics from a position of strict Christian morality.'[11] Of Josephine Butler it is written: 'Her belief in a loving God simply would not let her remain silent in the face of such injustice.'[12] This despite the moments of doubt referred to earlier.

Poverty and injustice abound in the far off lands of the developing world but they dwell much closer to home as well. We have all encountered the homeless in our cities, and when we do how do we react? Do we walk by on the other side like the priest and the Levite, or do we stop and talk like the Samaritan?[13] Are we in too much of a hurry to stop today? Have we discovered that the poor are not always overwhelmed with gratitude when we intervene on their behalf? That they might shout abuse at us, fail to keep an appointment or lie? Look in your heart and see what attitudes lie there, dormant unless provoked by a challenge. Justice for the poor and endangered, the fatherless and the orphans is one of the great golden threads of the Bible. To omit compassion, and its translation into some action on behalf of the poor, is to forgo fully living out our destiny. The Bible says that he who oppresses the poor shows contempt for their Maker, but whoever is kind to the needy honours God.[14] Elsewhere it tells us: '. . .faith by itself, if it is not accompanied by action, is dead'; and: 'Do not merely listen to the word, and so deceive yourselves. Do what it says.'[15]

During our years in Paris, I found that my answers to all those questions were revealed to be. . . Yes. . .and that, to my shame, my heart was full of fear and resentment about the poor. They didn't shape up when we helped them! They stole our blankets, they urinated at our front door and at our garage door (which became so corroded that it had to be replaced!); they smuggled alcohol into the Christmas party, and they urinated there in the church too; and they shouted at the person who was preaching. So what? So. . . our hearts were revealed to be seriously wanting. This last was an Angolan, who had seen his own family felled by gunfire in his homeland, somehow made his way to France, and turned to alcohol to treat the pain. He told us his name was 'le docteur Zaza', and perhaps, before pain drove him mad, he had indeed been a teacher as he claimed. He would sit quietly at the back of the church, but erupt unpredictably into a heart-rending plea, as he stumbled down the central aisle: 'Papa! Papa! Papa Charlie, je vous aime!' An interruption to a service? What about the time? Oh, but how we grew to love him, and our stony hearts slowly grew soft; towards him and towards the many poor whom we encountered.

When adults are poor, children are too. In 2004, 2.2 million children were living with HIV/AIDS;[16] 88 per cent of under 18s live in the developing world;[17] 246 million children are engaged in exploitative child labour;[18] there are 150 million street children worldwide;[19] and so the statistics multiply.

We live in a global age. No longer can we plead ignorance as a reason for apathy. Poverty, plague, slavery and war are not happening by accident, and they demand a response.

Many agencies exist to respond; the catchphrase 'Think globally, act locally' was never better illustrated than by the launching at the beginning of 2005 of the Make Poverty History campaign. This is a coalition of more than 120 organisations, joining in a massive, concerted effort to tackle world poverty. The campaign calls on world leaders to pursue fair trade, cancel unpayable debts and provide more and better aid. The monthly debt repayment of many nations in the developing world exceeds what they receive as aid, so some of the wealthiest and most powerful nations are beginning to think globally and act locally.

Another arena urgently requiring reform today is the environment, for the relentless abuse of our eco-systems by the wealthy nations is inextricably linked to poverty. Poor communities inevitably put their surrounding environment under stress. In turn that stress impacts negatively on the lives of those communities, producing a vicious cycle. Nothing illustrated the link between the environment and poverty more starkly than the catastrophic tsunami of December 2004. The amplification of suffering in the wake of the tsunami came about because poverty had forced people to live in dangerous areas, thus increasing risk to life. Thanks to corruption, planning restrictions had been ignored and so the natural coastal defences such as coral reefs and mangrove forests had been destroyed to make way for the densely crowded and poorly constructed dwellings that we saw swept away like matchsticks by the hundreds. It will take a long time to forget the footage of Banda Aceh.

It is very much the issue of the moment, yet radical action is low on government agendas. It is also low on the majority of church agendas, for green issues have traditionally been left to secular evangelists. Not entirely though! The Christian global conservation movement Arocha—the Rock—was born in southern Portugal in 1983. Twenty years on it has established active projects in 16 nations and is gathering momentum as growing numbers of people wake up to the environmental crisis.[20]

Poverty, plague, slavery and war demand a response from

governments, NGOs and the church, but they demand a response from you and me too. The very best way to think globally and act locally is to ask, 'What can I do today?' What relief agencies and missions does your church support? What provision for the poor has been made in your town? Does the need exceed the provision? Could you be involved in helping with an existing project or setting something up?

During our first year at St Aldate's, about a dozen different people brought Isaiah 58 to our notice, each one saying in his or her own way that they felt drawn to reaching the poor in Oxford. More than this they felt that there was a call from God to make sure the walls of our newly refurbished church were permeable, and the doors open and welcoming to everyone. It is so easy for a church building to shut people out.

Since then, largely as the brainchild of the wife of an Anglican ordinand, several ministries have been initiated under the umbrella name of ACT![21] A mother and toddler group; a much-expanded prison visiting programme, visiting four prisons in all; a befrienders group, which seeks to befriend the lonely and isolated around the city; and an ex-offenders group. Currently the first steps towards setting up a pregnancy crisis centre are being taken.

All these things use up hours of prayer and thought and longing and planning. None of them has been birthed without struggle and often tears. But all of them carry intense joy with them too. Loosing the chains of injustice is part of our destiny, but a costly part. Jesus said that greater love could not be shown than by laying down our lives for our friends, and he referred to himself, but he was also giving us a mandate.

Patrick Macdonald is one young man who has recognised
and responded to this mandate. Himself fatherless from the
age of 12, Patrick's world was turned upside down when, at
17, he met individual homeless children on the streets of
Bogota, Columbia. The impact this made on him was so
great that he returned to England vowing to pour his life
into the relief of children at risk. Fourteen years later, Viva
Network, founded by Patrick in 1994, is a flourishing and
ever-expanding organisation that seeks to link agencies
working on behalf of children world-wide. In Patrick's
words, 'We are essentially a network of networks. . .Viva
could be called The International Association of Evangelical
Work Among Children in Need, and our aim is to link Christians working with such children around the world.'[22]

It all began with one child who broke Patrick's heart; one
child, with a life and a destiny of which he would in all likeli-
hood be robbed; and it is with this awe of each life being
crafted together within his or her mother that we must all
begin. Statistics, so plentiful today, will blunt our compassion as they overwhelm us, but the face of a single child
looking into our eyes will ignite it.

We may think we cannot do much, but too often it stops
us doing anything. A smile and a kind word are better than
nothing, and if our hearts are set on the pursuit of justice,
we may be surprised by how far we are taken. To what
extent are you free to rub shoulders with those whose existence is rough and difficult, who have lost their children or
partner or wife or husband, who live with a history of abuse
or violence or illness or addiction? Or have you somehow
created a cocoon that shields you from anything too sad or
shameful? I venture to suggest that unless we connect with

the poor and deprived in even the simplest way, we cannot connect with our destiny. Why not decide today to ask God how he is calling you to show his love to the poor, and join the nineteenth-century Reformers, the twentieth-century heroes and the justice-seekers at the dawn of the twenty-first century?

10

God's Retirement Plan is Out of this World

The destiny of heaven

There have been times when I think we do not desire heaven, but more often I find myself wondering whether, in our hearts of hearts, we have ever desired anything else.

(C. S. Lewis)

There's an old story that does the preaching rounds: heaven is where the food is French, the police are English, the love is Italian, and it's all organised by the Swiss; hell is where the food is English, the police are French, the love is Swiss, and it's all organised by the Italians. I don't think our caricatures of each other will be that simply enshrined for eternity!

Nor do I think the fancies of the Revd Sydney Smith will necessarily be indulged: 'My idea of heaven is eating pâté de foie gras to the sound of trumpets.' Nor yet do I think it will be where we finally get our own way as some wit has said: 'Heaven: A place where the wicked cease from troubling you with talk of their personal affairs, and the good listen with attention while you expound your own.' My first brush with heaven was when I waved goodbye so prematurely to Samuel, though I waved not with peace or confidence but with a raging heart.

> Do not go gentle into that good night,
> Rage, rage against the dying of the light.[1]

Dylan Thomas wrote these words of the death of his father, and raged for old men, wise men, good men, wild men and grave men. I raged for an infant who would never become a man. Something I theoretically believed in drew close, unpalatably close, and some thinking had to be done when the storm subsided.

Many writers and divines have expressed themselves on this subject, each articulating in his or her own way longings and feelings that in the end are perhaps inexpressible, for none of us knows much about the subject after all! C. S. Lewis writes the following:

All the things that have ever deeply possessed your soul have been but hints of it—tantalising glimpses, promises never quite fulfilled, echoes that died away just as they caught your ear. But if it should really become manifest—if there ever came an echo that did not die away but swelled into the sound itself—you would know it. Beyond all possibility of doubt you would say, 'Here is the thing I was made for.' We cannot tell each other about it. It is the secret signature of each soul, the incommunicable and unappeasable want, the thing we desired before we met our wives or made our friends or chose our work, and which we shall still desire on our deathbeds, when the mind no longer knows wife or friend or work. While we are, this is. If we lose this, we lose all. [2]

Of necessity the majority of what we can say about heaven has to be gleaned from apprehensions; and since man began to write he has sought to capture those apprehensions, be he poet, philosopher or theologian.

> We shall rest and we shall see, we shall see and we shall love, we shall love and we shall pray, in the end which is no end.[3]

> Bring us, O Lord God, at our last awakening into the house and gate of heaven. . .where there shall be no darkness or dazzling, but one equal light, no noise nor silence but one equal music. No fears nor hopes but one equal possession, no ends nor beginnings, but one equal eternity. . .[4]

For many, heaven will be the constant presence of Jesus more certainly known:

> Christ is the desire of nations, the joy of angels, the delight of the Father. What solace then must that soul be filled with that hath the possession of him to all eternity.[5]

There are others who have visions of an open heaven, like Handel, whose vision inspired the writing of the 'Hallelujah Chorus' at the end of *The Messiah*. And many others who testify to having glimpsed or visited heaven during a near-death experience. Some such stories are fanciful, some are more thought-provoking, some are arresting, but in any case no indisputable view of heaven can be constructed from such accounts since they are so subjective and personal.

One account that made an impact on us is that of Prossy Mulinde, first wife of John,[6] who died in 2000. . .for the second time. John recounted this tale to us one day as we sat in the lunch bar of a P&O ferry, crossing from Dover to

Calais; the contrast between our drab surroundings and the brilliance of heaven created an unforgettable memory.

In 1988, John, and a team which included Prossy were conducting an evangelistic campaign, praying much and knocking on doors; not altogether welcomed by the communities in Uganda where they were working. A prophecy was given that the Lord was far more interested in their availability than their activity; but that because they were not heeding this message, he was going to show them a sign to prove that he meant it. One night they cried out in prayer to the Lord for several hours, until someone found Prossy, bent over in prayer, leaning against the wall, but stone cold. She had not moved for a long time. Slowly they began to realise that she was dead and some began to wail and scream, responding to death in the conventional way. John pleaded with them to be quiet, fearing the noise would aggravate the people of the area. But they also knew they would be accused of killing her and began to pray earnestly for her life to return. It was now nearing midnight. The hours passed and the pleading continued, but Prossy remained motionless and cold. As dawn began to steal across the sky they realised they would need to report her death, and lay out the body in preparation for medical and legal inspection. No one in the group wanted or dared to undertake this, and in desperation John cried out from the depths of his being for the help of the Lord. His eyes were closed as he communed with his God.

Suddenly his body jolted as Prossy rose in a single movement from where she had been immobile for eight hours and fell into his outstretched arms. Her lips were moving weakly and, in shock and amazement, the group saw that she was alive. They brought her some water and after a time she whispered, 'I have received a grace from the Lord.' They were the only words she uttered for a week. She was about 21, and in the December of that year she and John were married, for John had come to a certainty that she was to be his wife in the very instant that he caught her risen body. For many years she would not speak of the experience, except to repeat that God had given her a grace. From this time on she consistently communicated the need for unity, and when she addressed the leaders of Trumpet Mission at a troubled time, they spent twelve hours at a stretch with her and it seemed the presence of God was heavy upon them; they were rooted to the place, each dealing deeply in their hearts with God and utterly unaware of his neighbour. Several came into full-time leadership at the church as a result of that day.

In the intervening years until Prossy's second death, she and John had four children, as well as adopting a street child, like so many Ugandans, and parenting the two children born to Prossy during her teenage years; years of terror and fleeing from the Amin and Obote regimes which had unleashed random violence and killing across the country. She had spent at least a year living wild and on the run.

She died the month before she was due to visit Europe and finally give testimony to her experience of seeing heaven opened. The message is preserved on tape; quite difficult to hear. Like many she speaks of light, but she also speaks of understanding salvation and its urgency and of being questioned about her life. To listen to it is at once sobering and motivating.

By far the surest insights about heaven, however, are to

be found in the Bible. There are five things I want to draw out as encouragements to us in our call to be people whose final destiny is heaven, and whose lives should be lived as pilgrims with that perspective, in the world but not of the world, as Jesus prays for his disciples in the High Priestly prayer of John 17.

The first is that heaven is another world, another dimension that is much more real than earth. This is quintessentially captured in the words of Aslan to Susan, Lucy, Edmund and Peter in *The Last Battle* by C. S. Lewis: '. . .you are—as you used to call it in the Shadowlands—dead. The term is over: the holidays have begun. The dream is ended: this is the morning. . .'

Today, disillusioned by the failure of modernism, materialism and technology to satisfy the cry of deep to deep in our spirits,[7] we are turning to the non-material world in our desperation. Heaven is in another dimension, and it is our true home, so it can succour us even as we make our pilgrim's progress through all the sloughs of despond and the lodgings at doubting castle of our days on earth. Heaven is in fact where we truly exist:

> We were made for God. Only by being in some respect like Him, only by being a manifestation of His beauty, loving kindness, wisdom or goodness, has any earthly Beloved excited our love. It is not that we have loved them too much, but that we did not quite understand what we were loving. It is not that we shall be asked to turn from them, so dearly familiar, to a stranger. When we see the face of God we shall know that we have always known it. . .in Heaven there will be no anguish and no duty of turning away from our earthly Beloveds. First, because we shall have turned already; from the portraits to the

Original, from the rivulets to the Fountain, from the creatures
He made lovable to Love Himself. But secondly, because we
shall find them all in Him. By loving Him more than them we
shall love them more than we do now.[8]

The Old Testament expresses this other-worldliness in
terms of geography; it is high up and holy, the dwelling
place of God. 'Lift up your eyes to the heavens;[9] 'even the
highest heaven, cannot contain you';[10] 'for as high as
the heavens are above the earth'.[11] This verse goes on to
compare the difference in altitude with the difference in
capacity to love. The same idea is repeated in Isaiah:

> For my thoughts are not your thoughts, neither are your ways
> my ways, declares the Lord. As the heavens are higher than the
> earth, so are my ways higher than your ways and my thoughts
> than your thoughts.[12]

All of this calls us to recognise that while the way we think
may be good, even clever, it is nothing in comparison with
the author of all thought. He can give us insight when we
least expect it or are most desperate for it.

Secondly, heaven is a place of communication and provision. When the ark is brought to the Temple that Solomon
has built, he prays to the Lord, 'Hear from heaven, your
dwelling place, and when you hear forgive.'[13] Speaking
through Isaiah, God declares, 'Heaven is my throne and the
earth is my footstool.'[14] In Jacob's dream at Bethel, he sees
a 'stairway resting on the earth, with its top reaching to
heaven. . . There above it stood the Lord. . .'[15] Heaven is a
place the Israelites know as a place that God speaks from,[16]
as when he gave the Ten Commandments to Moses. In
Jacob's dream God spoke from heaven, reiterating the

promise first given to his grandfather, that Canaan would be given to their descendants who would be like the dust of the earth.[17] It is also a place that God hears from,[18] and a place that God provides from; he told Moses that he would rain down bread from heaven for the grumbling people under Moses' charge.[19] The phrase 'bread from heaven' reminds us that Jesus is the Bread of life, and that man shall not live by bread alone. This can be real provision in a day when old boundaries have been uprooted and anything goes, just as it was for the wandering Israelites.

Thirdly, heaven is for children. We are told that heaven belongs to little children,[20] and that we can't gain entry to heaven unless we become like little children.[21] Small children are trusting, ingenuous, simple and easily pleased. They have not yet learned how to be proud, devious, self-seeking or manipulative. Jesus was always welcoming and giving his attention to people whom everyone considered a nuisance. So we can access the provision from heaven no matter how complex our request or our need, if we come like a child to our Father.

Fourthly, heaven is a reality that is revealed as the veil is drawn back. We see this several times in the Bible, either clearly stated as such or strongly implied. The only place in the Old Testament where it is expressly stated that heaven is revealed is at the beginning of the book of Ezekiel.[22] He proceeds to capture in words a series of the most fantastical sights and events that lie for us by definition in the realm of fantasy, for he is describing things that come from another dimension. It is interesting that Philip Pullman, in his powerfully successful trilogy, *His Dark Materials*, whose message is that God is an evil dictator, has drawn heavily on the images of Ezekiel for some sections of his novels, but his purpose is the very opposite of encouraging us to look forward to the certainty of heaven:

> 'Tell me then,' said Will, 'tell me about Metatron and what this secret is. Why did that angel call him Regent? And what is the Authority? Is he God?'
>
> He sat down, and the two angels, their forms clearer in the moonlight than he had ever seen them before, sat with him.
>
> Balthamos said quietly, 'The Authority, God, the Creator, the Lord, Yahweh, El Adonai, the King, the Father, the Almighty— those were all names he gave himself. He was never the creator. He was an angel like ourselves—the first angel, true, the most powerful, but he was formed of dust as we are, and dust is only a name for what happens when matter begins to understand itself. Matter loves matter. . .the first angels condensed out of dust, and the Authority was the first of all. He told those who came after him that he had created them, but it was a lie. . .And the Authority still reigns in the Kingdom, and Metatron is his regent.'[23]

This is one of the most outright challenges that has ever been made to the truth of the gospel and the nature of God and Christ. It should disturb us, but more than that, it should provoke us to a ruthless pursuit of truth.

By implication, other characters in the Bible have heavenly experiences; Moses disappears for 40 days up Mount Sinai to the accompaniment of signs including fire, darkness, gloom and storm;[24] the prophet Isaiah has an overwhelming vision in the Temple;[25] King Solomon and the priests, on the occasion of the ark being brought to the Temple, can't perform their service because the Temple is filled with a cloud which is the glory of the Lord, in other words his presence;[26] and Joshua encounters the commander of the army of the Lord at the moment of facing his most difficult test to date, namely the conquering of Jericho.[27] These are all instances of the touching of two worlds, the elision of two kingdoms.

With the advent of Jesus in the New Testament, heaven is opened again at his baptism, variously recorded in all four gospels as being opened or torn open to reveal the Holy Spirit descending on him in the form of a dove. A voice comes from heaven confirming the identity of Jesus. Similarly, although the language used is not that of being opened, heaven is clearly close as the skies grow black to herald the death of Jesus and the earth quakes. After the resurrection, the disciples see Jesus taken up into heaven.

Others see heaven opened; Paul speaks of being taken up into the third heaven, or paradise, and hearing inexpressible things. Perhaps referring to this, or maybe to his conversion experience on the road to Damascus, which cannot be excluded from this category of illustration, he later tells King Agrippa at Caesarea[28] that he has done all that he has done in obedience to the vision from heaven. Somehow, what Paul had seen in and from heaven had filled him with an incomparable courage that had led him through violent persecution, deprivation of all kinds and prison. It must have been an amazing and powerful vision!

Equally extraordinary is the record of the death of Stephen.[29]

Stephen, full of the Holy Spirit, looked up to heaven and saw the glory of God, and Jesus standing at the right hand of God.

'Look,' he said, 'I see heaven open and the Son of Man standing at the right hand of God.'

For Stephen, Paul, and pre-eminently Jesus, heaven touching earth announces the supernatural in terms of pain as
well as power. Mark Stibbe notes:

> When the Holy Spirit descended upon Jesus at his baptism like
> a dove, Jesus was enabled and empowered not only to perform
> signs and preach with authority. He was also anointed to give
> his life as a ransom for many. He was endowed with the power
> for martyrdom as well as miracles.[30]

Others have powerful visions of Jesus; Daniel sees a vision
following a 21-day partial fast, and the apostle John sees a
vision while in prayer on the Island of Patmos where he had
been exiled for his faith. Later on he says he saw heaven
standing open. In both cases it is interesting to note that
there was a pursuit of God: similarly, the Roman centurion,
Cornelius, described as a God-fearing man who cares for
the poor and is familiar with prayer, receives a message
from an angel: and this before becoming a believer in Jesus.

Lastly, Jesus brings the kingdom of heaven wherever he
is. He himself tells his hearers that the kingdom of heaven
is near, is at hand.

So what, after all, is this heaven? Well, it is where we belong, Paul tells us.[31] Our citizenship is in heaven, he says.

'We talk about heaven being so far away. It is within
speaking distance of those who belong there.'[32] It's the final
destiny of our mortal being but, at the same time, Jesus
makes it clear that eternal life begins on earth: 'Now this is
eternal life: that they may know you, the only true God,
and Jesus Christ whom you have sent.'[33]

Heaven is where the dwelling of God intersects with earthly existence. Of course it will be but intermittent until we go through the gate of death, but we can call on it and expect to see evidence of it during our lives; where the kingdom of heaven comes there is healing, forgiveness, reconciliation and the wiping away of tears. God is calling you to have a heavenly perspective, and to live out your days in the light of that perspective. In other words, he calls us to be those whose values are not rooted in anything that can't be taken with us when our days on earth are done. He calls people who care little for accruing wealth or reputation and for whom possessions are enjoyable but incidental, things they are stewarding rather than owning.

Writing to the Corinthians, Paul compares our human body to a seed and the body we will have when we are raised from the dead to the plant that grows from that seed. So he turns on its head our typical notion that things earthly are much more reliable and substantial than things heavenly. 'The body that is sown is perishable, it is raised imperishable. . .it is sown in weakness, it is raised in power'; then he repeats himself, as if doubting that we have really understood: 'For the perishable must clothe itself with the imperishable, and the mortal with immortality.'[34] Then, he says, repeating himself for the third time, it will be true that death will have been swallowed up in victory. These are wonderful verses, strengthened by being repeated three times; for one of the hardest things following the death of someone is to believe that these things are really true; that far from being gone, the person has really arrived.

In the summer of 2004, the son of a friend took his life very unexpectedly. He was 35. Receiving the news, I broke down; I think because the memory of my own cousin doing the same thing at about the same age swirled about me again. Outside there were tears, but inside there were screams of protest, as the chaos of complicated questions swam at me like a dense net that threatened to close in on me and inextricably entangle me. Not long afterwards, I met my friend and was absolutely stunned by her serenity. Here is her story:

God is a covenant-keeping God of mercy and grace. We underestimate God's sovereignty and faithfulness; nothing happens without God being there. He's never surprised, never caught out. I recently met to pray with an Armenian pastor friend of ours and his wife. During the prayer time the Lord showed me a picture of a broken heart. At the time Stephen had just moved out to his own home and things were going well for him. Also at that time the Lord drew my attention to scriptures concerning the protection our faith can lend to another's life. He reminded me of his covenant with Abraham, and of the promise of rest given through the book of Hebrews. He reminded me how important it is to have a clean heart and that even the guilty can escape,[35] through God's grace in our lives. And he reminded me that children can be sanctified through the faith of a parent, as it says in 1 Corinthians 7:14. It was this verse that God said he would continue to tell me until I received it. When Stephen died, I heard the question, 'Whose report will you believe? Will you be like the disciples at the foot of the cross feeling that everything on which they had staked their lives had failed, or like the disciples on the road to Emmaus who were transformed from utter defeat to radiant hope in an instant of recognition?' I have been given an incredible lightness of spirit and strength from God. A friend who was praying for us was shown a vision of Jesus with Stephen in his arms, and I heard the words, 'I'll show you this as many times as you need to see it.' I saw the thief on the cross, and knew that we have no idea what happens as earthly life ends. If God is a long time answering, you have no idea what he's doing. . .in the process of answering, he refines us.

She, the bereaved mother, has been and is a tower of strength to the many who were rocked by Stephen's death.

This is a rare but precious testimony to the truth of Paul's words, and if we know something of the place of heaven in our lives, both now and afterwards, we will be equipped to draw many near to Jesus and be a source of strength and comfort. Paradoxically, it is through our weakness and brokenness that this strength so often comes. Without this experience of death coming so near, my friend would not have been able to comfort her son's distraught friends. I too know that I will see Samuel again one day, but I could not write about heaven if he had not been wrenched from me so suddenly.

Be sure that the ins and outs of your individuality are no mystery to Him; and one day they will no longer be a mystery to you. The mould in which a key is made would be a strange thing, if you had never seen a key; and the key itself a strange thing if you had never seen a lock. Your soul has a curious shape because it is a hollow made to fit a particular swelling in the infinite contours of the divine substance, or a key to unlock one of the doors in the house with many mansions. For it is not humanity in the abstract that is to be saved, but you—you, the individual reader, John Stubbs or Janet Smith. Blessed and fortunate creature, your eyes shall behold Him and not another's. All that you are, sins apart, is destined, if you will let God have His good way, to utter satisfaction. . .your place in heaven will seem to be made for you and you alone; because you were made for it—made for it stitch by stitch, as a glove is made for a hand.[36]

PART 3

11

Goaded By Guilt

The destiny of being forgiven

In the months following Samuel's death, I suffered frequent bouts of guilt. Different images would invade my imagination and cause me to wince, sometimes to physically recoil, and my stomach to contract. Nearly always, these images would provoke anguished sobbing. What were they?

I would see Samuel lying alone on the floor of a bedroom at a conference centre, arching his back and screaming; a tiny baby who could neither crawl nor walk, yet who managed in his discomfort to turn a full 360 degrees in the space of half an hour. We had gone, in the first week of our Californian visit, to a conference up in the mountains and I had made a bed for Samuel on the floor, having no Moses basket or travel cot. This was obviously the safest place to leave him, but how could I have left him at all, however short the time? Why had I not simply carried him in my arms to the session? I had chosen to be more interested in what someone was saying than in my new and precious son. Did something that I could have prevented happen to him during that half hour? By holding him to me and rocking him, I could have calmed his agitation, reduced the frenetic expenditure of his energy, and perhaps prevented him from becoming too weak to overcome what lay ahead.

I would see Samuel, screaming in the aeroplane cot that lay on the table just inches away from me, and myself, lying back in my seat, exhausted. Why didn't I realise he was dehydrating? Why didn't I drink more water myself? Why didn't I give him water?

I would see a hot stuffy changing room in a clothes shop in Bristol, where I was squeezing my post-natal body into a truly horrible trouser suit, because I thought I needed new clothes for the trip to America. Why didn't I stay at home with my newborn son, the answer to my prayers, who was so much more fulfilling than any new clothes could ever be? When I got home, he was distressed, and if I hadn't gone out, he wouldn't have been.

I would see myself holding a bottle of powdered baby milk that I had made up in desperation for Samuel. He seemed to be perpetually hungry. My milk seemed watery and in short supply. It was the only bottle of milk he ever had. Did it kill him? Ravi Zacharias, evangelist and author of many books, says this:

> What a vortex of human emotion swirls around this subject of guilt! We come up against it in our families. We battle for it in our courtrooms. We philosophize about it in the classroom. We try to explain it with psychology. We shout about it from the pulpit. We wrestle with it in private. So pervasive and deep-seated are its ramifications that some in professional counselling have gone so far as to say that guilt is the cornerstone of all neuroses.[1]

We have various responses to guilt. The first is to be persuaded that it doesn't exist. Our postmodern culture, in which there are no longer any absolutes, no boundaries, and whose philosophy is that we may believe, say and do as we like, provided we do no harm to another, tends towards the notion that guilt is imaginary and completely unnecessary. If right and wrong are purely subjective notions, I can claim not to be guilty when my behaviour troubles you, because I am being faithful to my personal creed. Yet we all know that, while we may subscribe to this because it seduces us with its promise of freedom, it raises problems. Recently in Britain we have lowered the age of consent for homosexuals to 16. Why should we not therefore in time, as our understanding of freedom grows, lower the age of consent for both heterosexuals and homosexuals to 14, to 12? If the child is consenting, there is logically no problem. Yet we all know there is a problem, because to be human is to recognise certain universal truths that supersede time and culture, which means that we do not operate solely on the basis of logic. To deny the existence of guilt will only imprison us more securely.

So, though we may wish to deny the existence of guilt, we know at a deep subconscious level that it is there. It is one of the earliest issues raised in the Bible. Having succumbed to the temptation to eat the one thing that was out of bounds, two things immediately happened to Adam and Eve in consequence. First, instead of being entirely comfortable with their nakedness as previously, they became embarrassed and ill at ease and spent the afternoon initiating the world of fashion by making designer fig leaf outfits. Disobedience had spawned shame. With shame comes disgrace, says the book of Proverbs. Hearing the Lord approaching as evening fell, they hid. I'm sure they didn't discuss what to do; guilt triggered their spontaneous reaction. And so we hide from the One who will demand an explanation.

Centuries later, King David, mighty general, lover of God, and forebear of Jesus, allowed an idea to take root in his mind as he strolled on his roof in the evening sun and caught sight of the beautiful Bathsheba bathing on another rooftop. An overpowering desire took hold of him, and he knew he could use the power of his position to transform it into reality. James writes that, after desire has conceived, it gives birth to sin, and sin, when it is full-grown, gives birth to death. In the story of David and Bathsheba, the first death that is caused is that of Bathsheba's husband, Uriah. David needs to conceal his paternity of the child now awaited as a result of his desire.

Unmasked by the prophet Nathan, a terrible remorse seizes David as he acknowledges his guilt. 'I have sinned against the Lord.' In Psalm 51, he pleads for mercy, asking to be washed and cleansed, wishing to be whiter than snow, and likening his pain to that caused by the breaking of bones. To admit guilt is to admit the possibility of wrongdoing; wrongdoing against a higher law than our own. In a culture that has tried to dispose of God, we can then begin to understand a profound resistance to the notions of guilt and sin. David knows that he has sinned against several people; Uriah, Bathsheba, their baby, his household; even the army out fighting the enemy on his behalf. But he knows too that his principal sin is against the law of God, and that it is from God that he must first seek forgiveness.

This he finds, but Nathan prophesies the consequences of

what has happened; the baby will die as well as Uriah; next, someone close to him, unidentified at this point, will commit adultery with his wives, and calamity will come upon him out of his own household. Seldom, if ever, can we claim that our choices affect only ourselves. It is important that we understand that forgiveness does not ensure a fairy-tale life; good actions have good consequences and bad actions have bad consequences as so strikingly illustrated in the life of David. But before we explore the workings and benefits of forgiveness, we need to recognise that there are other ways in which we deal with guilt.

A second way that is increasingly used to dispose of guilt is to mock and belittle Christianity. The media act as an effective vehicle for this, and we might say that a church which repeatedly fails to stand up for integrity, honesty and dignity has only itself to blame. One can think of a dozen documentaries, soaps and series that surreptitiously invade and influence our thinking. If faith and morality are meaningless and ridiculous, we are unlikely to be disturbed by the faint discomfort of guilt.

This reached a zenith with the broadcasting on BBC 2 in January 2005 of *Jerry Springer: the Opera*. It generated miles of print, both prior to and after the screening, and occupied as much air space. The most honourable offering in all this for me came from Antony Pitts, who was a Senior Producer for BBC Radio 3 until he resigned as a result of this broadcast. He describes how he was persuaded by Mark Thompson, the Director-General of the BBC, to watch the show before acting, although he had flagged up that many news sources[2] had made it clear that the show contained elements that were clearly blasphemous in any ordinary understanding of the word. His conclusion after watching it was that, 'the blasphemy was far, far worse than even the most detailed news reports had led me to believe'.

He cites some examples:

- The introduction of and dialogue with the Jesus figure containing all kinds of abuse, insults, profanity and deliberate mockery of the Lord's Name.
- The ridiculing of the figure of Jesus on the cross, dressed to imply sexual perversion.
- The repeated mockery of the wounds (stigmata) of Jesus, linked to acts of crudeness.
- The singing of 'Jerry eleison' as a contemptuous travesty of an act of worship.

He goes on to write out the current legal definition of blasphemy:

> Every publication is said to be blasphemous which contains any contemptuous, reviling, scurrilous or ludicrous matter relating to God, Jesus Christ or the Bible, or the formularies of the Church of England as by law established.[3]

This definition covers the written and spoken word.

He ends his letter of resignation by quoting the Latin inscription on Broadcasting House:

> This Temple of the Arts and Muses is dedicated to Almighty God by the first Govenors of Broadcasting in the year 1931, Sir John Reith being Director-General. It is their prayer that good seed sown may bring forth a good harvest and that the people, inclining their ear to whatsoever things are beautiful and honest and of good report, may tread the path of wisdom and uprightness.

And he signs off, 'My prayer is Kyrie eleison. Lord, have mercy.'

So far have we departed from this noble dedication that it is not in the least surprising that the nation that feasts on such spectacles should feel absolutely no need to be accountable to such a God.

A third way we smother guilt is by justifying our actions. How we are perceived by others is for most people an all-consuming cause and leads us often to sail close to the wind where truth is concerned. One of the best examples of this is to observe the public enquiry that follows a political scandal such as the one provoked by the death of Dr David Kelly, the civil servant believed to have been the source of leaked reports relating to the Iraq war in 2003. Several reputations were ruined, but there were no admissions of failure or guilt.

In the book of Samuel, we find Israel's first king, Saul, who has received clear instructions from God through the prophet and priest, Samuel, modifying those instructions according to his own understanding. Saul's excuse is that he took plunder from the enemy in the form of sheep and cattle, in order to sacrifice them to the Lord, but a few verses earlier we have been told that he kept everything that was good, while destroying everything that was weak and despised. When Samuel calls his bluff and utters the unforgettable words, 'To obey is better than to sacrifice. . .rebellion is like the sin of divination, and arrogance like the evil of idolatry,[4] announcing that Saul's kingship is over, Saul admits that he has sinned, and that it was because he was afraid of the people. He asks for forgiveness and to resume his kingship, but in a dramatic scene, Samuel says it is too late and turns to leave. We may imagine his robes whirling as he turns, and tearing as Saul grasps at them, revealing a man who could not hear the word of the Lord.

> You have rejected the word of the Lord, and the Lord has rejected you as King over Israel. . .The Lord has torn the kingdom of Israel from you today, and given it to one of your neighbours—to one better than you.[5]

Of course this is not the first time that Saul has overridden Samuel's instructions. Not long before this incident, he had acted as priest, which was not his role, and been rebuked by Samuel in a similar way. He had also shown early signs of his deep sin of jealousy when his son Jonathan had achieved a great victory for the Israelites. Later he became uncontrollably jealous of Jonathan's friendship with David and of David himself. Saul was a person who repeatedly tried to cover up his guilt, and it led in the end to his death. The frightening thing about his exchange with Samuel, in which he learns that the kingship is to be taken away from him, is that his last thought concerns what others think of him. I have sinned, he says; but please honour me before the elders of my people, and before Israel. Please maintain my reputation even if it is a whitewashed tomb. The final verse of that chapter says that the Lord was grieved that he had made Saul king over Israel. Let's reflect on this incident for a moment. This man cared far more about the opinion of men than the opinion of God. He had smothered his guilt in that greatest of all sins, pride. C. S. Lewis expresses this well:

> You may remember, when I was talking about sexual immorality, I warned you that the centre of Christian morals did not lie there. Well, now we have come to the centre. . .the utmost evil

is pride. Unchastity, anger, greed, drunkenness, and all that are mere fleabites in comparison. It was through pride that the devil became the devil. Pride leads to every other vice: it is the complete anti-God state of mind.

Yet another way in which we deal with guilt is by concealing rather than denying it, and living in fear of discovery. We hide it by appearing to be in control. Thus we cannot go very far in friendship, because if we do we may be discovered and we will certainly have to disclose ourselves. Abraham's grandson Jacob is a perfect example of a devious life, from wheeling and dealing with his brother to tricking his elderly father and scheming against his father-in-law.[6] Deceiving his father led to wronging a nation, because deceit is a monster that needs feeding, and to hide guilt will always have repercussions on others as we create a web of lies to cover our tracks. Deceiving his brother meant he had to flee and lose contact for many years, being absent at his mother's death: and when eventually the moment of confrontation between the estranged brothers arrived, Jacob was in anguish all night, wracked with fear before God that the wrong he had committed so long ago would be avenged against his children.

Jacob found mercy because he came to God; thousands don't because they have neither looked for nor found him, or they have believed the lies of our culture. Christianity is the only world religion whose voice cries out for people to deal with sin, to admit guilt, ask for pardon and come to God to receive it. But its voice is growing faint in a culture that is casting off all restraint and pro-actively seeking to silence the voice of Jesus.

Living through those early months after Samuel's death, I knew the reality of guilt. While I was assured repeatedly by paediatricians and other medical authorities with whom we automatically came into contact, both immediately following his death and later when I became pregnant with Jack, that I was not responsible for what had happened, I knew that there were moments of inadequacy as a mother, as exemplified by some of the scenes rehearsed at the beginning of the chapter. These things were not to do with legalities; they were not subject to human judgement. They were rather a question of conscience between me and my God. In what way might this affect the next generation walking into their destiny?

I have spoken to numerous parents of the pain of seeing their children walk away from the Lord, but who in their pain have responded with a sense of resignation. It has become God's problem, and they hope and pray that one day the child will return. There is almost unbearable pain in seeing a child suffer, whatever the cause. Of course, we cannot make an equation: I did this so my son did that. But behind resignation can lie an awareness and acceptance that somewhere along the line, because we ourselves as parents are damaged and bruised, we may be partly responsible. In a way it would be strange to think otherwise. But our culture has persuaded us that this can't be so, and we feel guilty for ever feeling the slightest twinge of guilt.

I want to make a plea for guilt to become part of our parenting; that is, for us to openly admit that we may bear some responsibility for the stories in which we find ourselves. Perhaps this seems scandalous in a culture which denies or suppresses guilt. But that's not the end of the story; if we turn to the heart of the gospel and ask ourselves why Jesus submitted to the agony of the cross, we remember that the answer is to provide a way for us to find peace with God. To bear away our sins. To pay the debts we could never pay ourselves. To enjoy the destiny and freedom of forgiveness.

Jean Vanier, the founder and director of L'Arche, an international ministry for the handicapped, with whom he worked, lived and learned how to love, writes: 'The yearnings of Jesus. . .are to undo the chains that bind us up in guilt and egoism, and prevent us from walking on the road to inner freedom and growth.'

If we will but let these misgivings tumble out of us and say, 'Yes, I didn't recognise those teenage confusions; yes, I was too strict about your clothes; yes, I did allow my anger to lacerate your soul when you weren't even really the cause of it. My work situation, my relationship with your father at the time, my fatigue all demolished my self-control; I was so wrong; please forgive me': then we will find not resignation but resolve waiting for us.

What so often happens is that the spring of prayer within us dries up because we have not felt that a confession of guilt is appropriate. And we have been encouraged by our culture, and sadly so often by the church as well, in this conclusion. The fruit of all this is multiple. There is alienation between the generations; thousands of young men and women wander in the wilderness for far too long because we have adopted the false theology that we can do nothing except wait. And thousands of children, while growing up surrounded by other Christians and immersed in church culture, are passengers rather than passionate, because they don't feel forgiven for their teenage tantrums, they hear gossip and criticism of others, and they see lengthy disputes conducted through the medium of interminable meetings that in addition deprive them of their parents' time. The pleasure and the glory of forgiveness are hidden from us because we have been persuaded that we do not need it.

I had to verbalise my sense of guilt about Samuel's death and my shortcomings as his mother with Charlie and with friends before I could come to a place of peace.

Part of the road back to wholeness for my daughter Hannah involved my recognising how little of her struggles I had truly understood; the extent that I had expected her to be more mature than her years; the subconscious expectations I had laid on her as a pastor's daughter (because of what people would think of us); the pain I had inflicted through my frequent outbursts of anger. I may have been in pain, but pain does not justify anger, nor striking out in uncontrollable rage. . .and wasn't there the nagging feeling of guilt lurking behind all this because we had torn her from her home and nation at the vulnerable age of 14 and expected her to feel as excited as we did? I had to confess all of these things to God, and I had to confess all of these things to her. I had to ask both of them for forgiveness, and they both granted it. I doubt if I could write about guilt if these things had not happened.

I can still see Jack flinching as I raised my hand threateningly. We had a volatile relationship during those teenage years of his in Paris. Like the majority of teenagers, he would while away hours listening to music (not very suitable music!) and doodling when he was meant to be doing 'les devoirs'. Neither reasoning nor persuading nor cajoling seemed to produce any reaction, so I resorted to physical persuasion with him too. I say this to my shame, but I say it because I know I am not alone. I am not alone as a parent, and I am not alone as a Christian. I did it because I was afraid. I was afraid he would not be able to reintegrate into the British education system when the time came. We all have different fears, but not one of them justifies being violent with our children. We had always practised saying sorry as soon as possible in our family, but asking for forgiveness for the same thing too often weakens the ability to forgive, and a time came, some years later, when I had to have a conversation with Jack and wrap up the business of the guilt I felt concerning this turbulent period of our common life.

The pain of all this was only mitigated by the sweetness of forgiveness which had freed me to pray for him with energy and passion. If we suppress our guilt as parents, whatever method we choose to obliterate it, so will our children. We are, after all, their role model.

Once, at a weekly student meeting at St Aldate's, the theme of the evening was learning to pray for one another. It was more a workshop than a teaching, and those of us on the team wandered around the groups to offer help or advice if needed. I asked one girl what she had asked for prayer for. Sex and lust, she replied. In your head or your body, I asked. Both, came the answer. I found out that she was a Christian and made an appointment with her. Without a place to admit guilt, make confession and receive forgiveness, where might this sweet young thing end up? Not fulfilling her destiny, that is certain.

Charles Spurgeon wrote, 'We are certain that there is forgiveness, because there is a gospel, and the very essence of the gospel lies in the proclamation of the pardon of sin.' Part of our destiny is to liberally ask for forgiveness, and to give and receive it. It is worth pointing out that the system often breaks down, not because we have done away with guilt, but because we can't forgive ourselves. Is our sin simply too big or complicated for even God himself to handle? Nothing is beyond the reaches of his forgiveness, and if God forgives us, who are we to withhold forgiveness from ourselves?

'It is always the case that when the Christian looks back, he is looking at the forgiveness of sins.'[7] Sometimes those who have the greatest perceived need of forgiveness are those who best understand it. Luke 7 recounts the story of the sinful woman (which means prostitute) who came to the Pharisee's house where Jesus was having dinner and knelt weeping at his feet, drying them with her hair and pouring perfume on them. How very inappropriate and embarrassing! What exactly is your relationship with this woman? And how extremely rude to gatecrash our dinner party. But she who had so little had so much for she knew that forgiveness was her only hope and she had found out where to get it.[8] As this same story reveals, the more we are forgiven, the more grateful we are, and the more loving we become, for we are amazed to be acceptable after what we have done. This story reminds me too of Ben, an ex-offender who has recently joined our congregation; a man who once did something terrible, but who exudes love because his life, like that of the sinful woman, has been turned inside out through meeting Jesus and finding forgiveness. There is logic as well as awe in the fact that the gospel thrives in prison. 'Forgiveness is the answer to the child's dream of a miracle by which what is broken is made whole again, what is soiled is again made clean.'[9]

So I wonder if you need to do something? Steer clear of email which can easily give the wrong message, but if you need to make a visit or a telephone call, or write a letter, go for it. It's a destiny decision.

12

Untimely Death

The destiny of living through death

I could tell from Charlie's tone as he answered the phone that something was terribly wrong. 'We need to go and see Dan and Suzie; the scan was bad.'

To their great joy, Dan and Suzie were expecting their third child, a little sister, they had already discovered, for older brothers Jack and Josh, now eight and six. Sitting in their kitchen minutes later we listened to them telling us that the scan had revealed that the left side of the baby's heart was grossly under-developed. This is Hypoplastic Left Heart Syndrome, an extremely rare condition with devastating implications. While in utero, and therefore dependant on the mother for sustaining life and providing nourishment, the baby thrives and will be as active as any normal baby. But from the moment of birth, when the baby becomes self-reliant for sustaining life, and therefore dependent on his lungs and heart, the clock is ticking and death is inevitable. The only question is how many days of life will be eked out by a failing organ.

Over the last 20 years surgery has been developed which can re-direct the flow of blood into and out of the developed half of the heart in order to sustain life. Even with surgery, no child suffering from this syndrome has yet lived beyond 15, and the doctors had clearly communicated, as they are obliged to, that quality of life is usually poor and the normal activities of a growing child such as running and jumping severely restricted.

Dan and Suzie had come home from what should have been a routine visit to the maternity hospital to face one of the most agonising questions a parent can ever have to face. The question before them was whether to subject a tiny, vulnerable infant to punishing and painful surgery in the hope of giving her a chance to live a life, with no guarantee that it would be easy or prolonged, or whether to allow her to drift away to eternity after her birth without surgical intervention in however many days it took. They had time to think about it, but this made it no easier.

Today they were in no state to do any thinking. Like us, many years earlier, their world had been turned upside down in a matter of minutes. The first signs that something was terribly amiss had been the sudden influx of medical staff into the room where the scan was taking place and the look on the consultant's face. We sat clutching our cups of tea and weeping with them. Trying to grasp the enormity of the day's discovery, we prayed, but our voices felt faint and it was hard to find faith in the wake of so much medical information.

There followed four long and difficult months for Dan and Suzie. Their family and friends rallied round, and heaven was most certainly stormed by many on their behalf, but still it was a lonely path as they journeyed to a decision about what to do when little Jessica Rose was born. Trips to Great Ormond Street hospital and lengthy consultations with surgeons and specialists came and went; so did long conversations with friends and private times of prayer and wrestling together. In the end they opted for surgery. It seemed unthinkable to choose not to offer Jessica every possible chance to live a life on earth.

The birth was physically relatively easy, and Suzie was up within hours to go and join her little infant who had been whisked straight to Great Ormond Street. If the last four months of the pregnancy had been difficult, what followed was a much greater challenge. The operation was announced successful, though the sight of their daughter wrapped in cling film around her open sternum, since the little chest was too small to sew up immediately over the swollen heart with needles, tubes and monitors everywhere, was almost too much to bear. It was January 15th, and Jessica was three days old.

Long winter day succeeded long winter day, but slowly, so slowly, little Jessica recovered. The little heart kept beating. Three weeks later she was transferred to the John Radcliffe hospital in Oxford, and it was there that we first saw her. Tiny, pale, perfect and beautiful. Breathtaking. Another three weeks later, what had seemed impossible happened. Jessica went home. The family was reunited; Suzie was radiant; we all wept tears of joy, relief and amazement.

They had several weeks as a little family. Suzie brought Jessica to church, and one day I met her out shopping, the perfect little bundle with her bright eyes wrapped up warm in her pram. But on April 14th, another phone call came.

'Charlie, I have to tell you that Jessica died this morning.' No! No! NO! A familiar engulfing wave of rejection rose up from deep inside me; a powerful human emotion in which it's as if one's whole being is activated in some strange way to defend from danger. Truly, death is the last and greatest enemy. Jessica had finished a feed and simply and suddenly died as her heart ceased to beat. She was in her mother's arms.

A week later the church was packed with people who came to say goodbye. This was a truly momentous funeral. Just as we had declared all those years ago that God was not on trial, so, in different words, this eternal truth was again proclaimed. Dan chose to sing 'St Patrick's Breastplate'; a choice to declare his faith with defiance to any, human or spirit, who would sneer at a loving God in such a context. All were amazed by his clear and unfaltering voice which lanced our working hearts; for any who were present and unsure about God, this courageous act was a certain and wonderful goad. Suzie, pale but beautiful, spoke with authority, composed and serene. Every word counted. Among them were these: 'I used to say as a joke that I wanted a little girl so that I could plait her hair and buy her shoes. But I had time to do neither.' Charlie guided the grieving company through each part of the service: that the veil between heaven and earth, usually so sturdy, seemed but a film, was perhaps partly because his own heart knew dearly about such things. As the service came to an end, Dan and Suzie projected a photographic record of Jessica's life while the old song rang out:

> Not from sorrow, pain or care,
> Freedom dare I claim. . .
> This alone will be my prayer,
> Glorify your name.

If anyone had not been undone so far, they were now. For myself, the appearance of the little white coffin before the beginning of the service threw me in a way I was completely unprepared for. I did not know so much grief could still be inside me, but the wells of human emotion are very deep, and from time to time the cover is removed. The years rushed up in an instant to meet me and bring back that other far away funeral.

A question has lingered with me since that day; did Jessica fulfil more of a destiny in three short months than many a mortal who walks the earth for three score years and ten and (increasingly today) well beyond that? If it is true that before you were formed in the womb, God knew you, that before you were born you were set apart;[1] that all the days ordained for you were written in your book;[2] several thoughts follow. Firstly we might suggest that the quality of our life is more significant than the quantity. We live in a culture which has effectively put away death. Corresponding to a post-Christian age where there are no longer any common absolutes, there are fewer and fewer individuals who will profess themselves ready to die for the name of Christ, as the martyrs of old so readily did. From this we might suggest, secondly, that finding out what God set us apart for, what we have been made for, is of much greater importance than securing a well-ordered life and bank balance. Thirdly, we might question common definitions of happiness. Paul gives us an interesting perspective on this issue:

For me to live is Christ and to die is gain. If I am to go on living in the body, this will mean fruitful labour for me. Yet what shall I choose? I do not know! I am torn between the two: I desire to depart and be with Christ, which is better by far, but it is more necessary for you that I remain in the body.[3]

Not your average perspective in the West today! I recently met a friend of one of our daughters who has a large tattoo of a Huguenot cross on her back, with Paul's words, 'For me to live is Christ, to die is gain', inscribed in Greek around the outer edge of the circle. That tattooing is a controversial subject, or that the dove dives neatly into that intriguing spot that joins back to buttocks, I chose to ignore. I felt I was meeting someone who had connected with her destiny.

Of course we cannot deny that, in an age of terrorism, we witness the willingness of a number of people, mostly young, to lose their lives for the sake of a cause. We live in an age of an increasing number of extraordinary psychodramas, as Muslim extremists sometimes combine mediaeval barbarity with the Internet and behead random hostages when their equally random demands are not met. The whole world is holding its breath as we are drawn into war without rules whether we want to be or not. For the hostages caught up in these extraordinary events it is more, of course, a question of their destiny being cut short than of embracing death. But for those who do the cutting short, the hostage takers, clearly death is a welcome option should the opportunity present itself or should they lose control of the game. If this was not crystal clear to the world before 9/11, it has certainly been so since that day, universally regarded as a hinge of history. Perhaps the definitive difference between such 'martyrs' and those who die for their faith in Christ is captured by Paul: 'If I give all I possess to the poor and surrender my body to the flames, but have not love, I gain nothing.'[4]

Many are those whose lives have been cut short by accident, illness or assassination. We can think of David Brainerd who yielded his life to tuberculosis at the age of 29 after ministering to the American Indians for five years, from 1742–47. We can think of Martin Luther King, assassinated in his prime as he fought for racial justice and equality hundreds of years later in the 1960s. We can think of David Watson, to whom I referred in an earlier chapter, who succumbed to cancer at the age of 50; of John Wimber, notorious for his persevering stance on healing and practice of praying for it, who likewise died of cancer at the age of 67. The list is in fact endless, for history is liberally scattered with noble characters who inspire courage, devotion and admiration of all that can be most glorious in a human being. However, although this is a catalogue of those whose lives can be said to have been cut short, and though, had they lived on, they would certainly have added to their achievements, there is an unspoken consensus that in some way they fulfilled their destiny. Why do we think this? I venture to suggest that what the human spirit perceives in such persons is a reflection of the nature of Jesus, who supremely fulfilled his destiny in the space of 33 years. All these people have, to one degree or another, become mature, attaining to the whole measure of the fullness of Christ.[5]

If we turn to those whose lives have been snuffed out before they have barely begun, like Samuel and Jessica, the question becomes much more delicate and complex. It is in fact a question that cannot be answered: I don't know what the destiny of these two tiny infants was in terms of life on earth, but I do know that the loss of Samuel woke up my own soul to the realisation that I was here for a reason, not merely to live out my days without focus or purpose. Many are perhaps propelled into their destiny by just such a tragedy striking their life. It is like an alarm bell sounding, putting us on alert and leading into a search for the meaning of our life. So one person's destiny might be activated by the cutting short of another's; the death and resurrection of Jesus catapulted a bunch of men who were slow to grasp what was going on, from the feeding of the five thousand to the transfiguration, into a group of powerful evangelists, preachers and prophets.

Every tragedy has the potential to open up or close down the destiny of others. The death of someone we love crushes, paralyses and immobilises us; it empowers doubt, releases hopelessness, robs us of energy and makes us sit down by the wayside in tears and give up. A graphic picture of such dejection was one sealed in the memory of many during the 2004 Olympics: the sight of the marathon runner Paula Radcliffe sinking to the ground, later saying, 'There was just nothing in my legs.' A good description of the physical manifestation post trauma. After the death of Samuel, I felt like this for a long time. But in this period of what feels like a suspension of life itself, something was taking place at a deeper level. This disruption of my former plans would not be allowed to crush my spirit and make me give up on that for which I believed myself to be called, namely to accompany Charlie on the lifelong task of building whatever local expression of church we found ourselves called to at different stages of our life. One might assume that tragedy, whether clothed in death or other garments, would stifle faith and energy to trust God and believe he can hear our cries. So often it does the very opposite.

During our time in Paris, we met the Beise family. Jim and Angela first came to Paris with their baby, Brian, to work with Youth With A Mission in 1987. While living in Paris they had their second and third children, Melissa and Rachel. Returning to the States to further their training, their fourth child, Michael, was born. Michael was born with a composite of handicaps.

They began a journey of multiple operations for Michael, disrupting their family life and taking them on a very different route from the one they had imagined. Nevertheless they decided to return to France all the same, and arrived in 2000.This was not going to divert what they understood to be their destiny. Meeting Michael and watching the dynamics of this extraordinary family provoked further questions over the subject of destiny. Michael cannot be said to be living what most of us would deem a normal life, and nor can his family; yet the tapestry of this family's communal life is far richer and more filled with meaning and purpose than many a family life untroubled by such a challenge. Could it be that Michael is in fact fulfilling his destiny and that, because of him, so is his family, and many others who come within their orbit and are brought up short by what they see in this family?

In 2003, Angela sent me the following piece of writing about Michael:

Recently my son Michael's therapist/teacher said something to me that shook me to the core of my being. It took me a few days to process her comment and to begin to understand my own reaction. Michael is eight years old [6] and has a rare genetic syndrome called 18Q-minus. We moved to France three years ago, with our four children to work as missionaries. We have been surprised to find that there are few schools for disabled children, and none where they can be mainstreamed. In our area of Paris alone there are 300 handicapped children on a waiting list for a school place. We have searched in vain for three years for a place for Michael. Fortunately we have a teacher who comes to our home twice a week to teach him.

On this occasion we were talking as she left our house after a therapy session about this question. She has been pro-active in helping us in our search, and was telling me about a couple of schools in the area that exist specifically for children with Down's Syndrome. She encouraged me to apply, although Michael does not have Down's. Then she made the shocking, or what should be shocking statement. 'Schools for Down's Syndrome children are starting to take children with other syndromes, since Down's is becoming so rare. Now that tests can tell so early in pregnancy that a baby has Down's, fewer people are choosing to complete the pregnancy.' I walked back into my house trying to unscramble my reaction to her statement.

Michael has benefited greatly from the incredible advances in medical technology. He was born with a cleft lip and palate, and feet that required extensive surgery. I am grateful for amazing doctors, and technology, that have so beautifully met his needs. But today I wondered whether technology was also robbing us of an important element of society.

In the days that followed I tried to imagine a society void of disabled people. What if this technology reaches a stage at which any or all babies with special needs can be eliminated? What would society look like if everyone were 'normal', if we never had to make provision for people who are slow, or deaf, or blind, or lame, or crippled? What if we could eliminate the 'weak' altogether? The question that haunted me was this: Do disabled, imperfect people contribute anything to society? Do we need them in order to be balanced, healthy and whole?

I didn't have to look any further than my own family to start finding answers. My children are among the most selfless, giving people I have ever known. I am in awe of them. They have made sacrifices, too numerous and too big to calculate, for their handicapped sibling. One might think that this would make them bitter and discontented with life. In fact it has done exactly the opposite. They are thankful and giving, and tolerant of difficult and unlovely people. Could it be that these 'imperfect' people somehow balance society as a whole? How would love and compassion be developed among people who were exclusively surrounded by beautiful and intelligent people? My children treasure nothing more than a smile or kiss, sometimes just eye contact from their little brother. Sometimes I see my husband kiss our son's often expressionless, crooked little face and my heart nearly bursts with a love and joy I can hardly contain.

As I continued to ponder the future with its possibility of a 'perfect' society, a verse from the Bible kept coming to mind. 'Do nothing out of selfish ambition or vain conceit.'[7] I can think of no other reason to eliminate a disabled child than either of these things. To parent a disabled child will require many ambitions to be laid aside. Large sums of money may have to be spent on therapists, doctors, medical bills and equipment. The child will become the focus of most of your time and energy and will determine what you can and cannot do in many situations. He can bring limitations to the dreams you can pursue. He can bring more sleepless nights than most parents will ever have to endure. Parenting seasons will be unusually long, and grief will last the lifetime of such a child. Parents not only grieve the child they 'lost' at his birth but grieve as they watch him struggle with tasks that normally come easily to a child of his age. They grieve when he realises he is not like other children, and when they see him in physical or emotional pain. They will certainly die to selfish ambition.

What about vain conceit? That will die too. It's often embarrassing to have a child who cries out in public for no reason, doesn't always behave appropriately in social settings, looks different, and acts differently. He will never be top of the class, or a good athlete. Most of what this child's parents will do will be for the benefit of another individual.

I wonder if in time when our advanced technology has succeeded in eliminating the weak and needy, whether our scholars, theologians, poets and politicians won't ponder the question: How did our society become so selfish and loveless, so intolerant and so driven by individual gain? Will the 'perfect' society be a place where any of us would want to live.

I am one parent of a child with special needs who is better because this child came into my life. Would I have chosen this road? Never in a million years. Am I grateful for the changed person I am today? You bet. Would I trade one sleepless night, hour in a hospital, penny spent on medical bills, or minute spent in a therapist's office? No chance. All heartache considered, I'll take the 'imperfect' society.[8]

The current evolution of British and European law in this area poses a threat to the fulfilment of destiny; Joanna Jepson, ordained in the Church of England, was operated on for a cleft palate as a baby, and gained notoriety following her high profile campaign many years later to bring abortion back into the national arena for debate. Her reason was that, had her life begun at a different time, it might not have begun at all. Some say she is a front-runner as candidate for a bishopric one day. Her life surely has the marks of destiny upon it.

The concept of destiny is too vast, philosophical and complex for us fully to comprehend it, and theologians from Augustine to Barth have analysed, expounded and pronounced on the subject. My goal is to raise rather than answer questions and provoke you to desire to live a life that is full of adventure and compassion. I believe that God lovingly creates every human being to walk through an exciting and unique existence on the earth with him. Equally, I believe that because the world has refused his leadership and lordship, multitudes are wandering in the desert, without focus, without purpose and searching unsuccessfully and increasingly despairingly for meaning in a world that grows more dangerous as it grows more sophisticated. Thus they are bypassing what they are appointed for.

You have a particular destiny, you are called to purpose and life in all its fullness, which is what Jesus said he had come to give.[9] Let yourself be inspired by the stories of martyrs and heroes, of men and women who were longing for a better country, a heavenly one,[10] and so were free from the various forms of slavery in which this world so often imprisons us. Every day is unique and every day counts. Three decades redolent with purpose and meaning better describe destiny than six without. Let yourself be inspired even by the little ones that spent so short a time on earth yet made such an impact upon their parents and many others. Let yourself be inspired by the brief life of Jessica and the unfinished story of Michael, and let them draw you to seek out and live your destiny.

13

A Loaf of Bread

The destiny of healing and wholeness

I was introduced to Laura by our vicar. There was a background that made it more suitable for me to help, it seemed. I soon found out why. Laura was attending an Alpha Course,[1] although she had decided that Christianity was the way for her some years previously. Now she had completed her training as a nurse and was working part-time. She spent the rest of her time earning a considerably higher salary as a sex worker. She had met and fallen in love with John at college. She had also fallen into bed with him, and sadly there is nothing very shocking or even very unusual about this, even within the ranks of the churched. One thing led to another, and Laura soon discovered that John was working as a male escort and becoming an increasingly wealthy property owner from the proceeds. Now seduced rationally as well as physically, she had entered the world of sex work under John's tuition and was doing rather well herself, owning one house in Oxford and renting another out to students: students we can assume who were blissfully ignorant of the financial affairs of their land-lady.

Laura saw no contradiction between her work and being a Christian. Indeed she became rather annoyed if I posed questions on Christian morality, and told me repeatedly what a lot of good she was doing, bringing a few moments of intimacy and comfort to a succession of mostly lonely men in their fifties. She insisted she was completely un-affected emotionally, and described to me her very business-like approach: a room set aside exclusively for this work in her house; its own sets of linen and towels and so on. She conveyed the impression of a very clean and tasteful busi-ness. She was only 23 years old, the same age as one of my daughters. We met for six sessions of studying the Bible together, because despite her assurances that she was con-tented with life and in love with John, there was a quest to find a love that is much safer. She had, because of her ear-lier experiences of growing up with believing parents, some inklings of this true love, and perhaps they were sounding from deep within her, reminding her of a far-off place and awakening a universal nostalgia. But she was feisty and argumentative; committed to nit-picking the text of John's Gospel and striving to reconcile it with her chosen way of life. At the same time, there was part of her that longed to settle down in a more conventional way with John, and she was prepared to go to any lengths to secure such a future: except the lengths that demanded she confront his lifestyle.

One Sunday she brought John to St Aldate's. He lived in London and was also attending a church where some were building bridges of love and friendship with him in an admirable way. Laura warned me to be careful what I said to him. I forget now my actual words, but they were not received in the way they were offered and, unwittingly causing offence, the game was lost. From that moment on, Laura became unreachable on her mobile and invisible in church and, after several weeks of leaving messages, I gave up the chase.

I have no idea what happened to John or Laura. Would that they had both integrated into the church he was attending at the time in London. I am far from a perfect communicator; I am sure my words could have been more carefully chosen: but I am sure too that they fell on the ears of one so insecure that the chances of being misinterpreted were high if not inevitable.

They were a sweet but ensnared couple, typical in many respects of so many of their generation. Paul says that the body is not meant for sexual immorality, but for the Lord. 'Do you not know,' he continues, 'that your bodies are members of Christ himself? Shall I then take the members of Christ and unite them with a prostitute? Never! Do you not know that he who unites himself with a prostitute is one with her in body? For it is said, "The two will become one flesh."'[2]

By this he shows his understanding that the sexual act represents much more than bodily union, and that to become one flesh with someone has consequences well beyond the relatively short time it takes to do so.

All down human history man's sexual appetite has caused him to over indulge, so to speak; there is barely a hero of whatever realm of society or whatever epoch, whose biography does not include amorous escapades and adventures.

After the self-restraint imposed by the years of the Second World War, there grew up a generation who revolted against their parents' hypocritical observance of a Victorian moral code and, casting all caution to the winds, threw themselves into the permissive society.

Defining events in the corporate life of that generation, the so-called Baby Boomers legitimised a new code of conduct. Woodstock, the New York upstate concert in 1969, was one of those events, ratifying free love in the collective consciousness, though other landmarks had appeared earlier. The poet laureate Philip Larkin puts it thus:

> Sexual intercourse began in
> Nineteen sixty-three
> (Which was rather late for me) —
> Between the end of the Chatterley ban
> And the Beatles' first L.P.[3]

The end of the Chatterley ban refers to the result of the Old Bailey obscenity trial launched in 1960 when Penguin Books decided to publish D. H. Lawrence's erotic novel, *Lady Chatterley's Lover* in paperback, thus putting an effective end to the censorship that had forced its publication abroad.

At the same time the rising star of the Beatles was a significant element in the establishing of a profound cultural change that would irrevocably influence the nation's moral opinions, leading us eventually to today's state of almost total undress in art, culture, writing, theatre, cinema and fashion. These defining influences of the 60s are captured by Ian MacDonald:

> As British Pop Art and Op Art became the talk of the gallery world, a new generation of fashion designers, models and

photographers followed Mary Quant's lead in creating the bou-
tique culture of swinging London. . .long-standing class barri-
ers collapsed overnight as northern and cockney accents
penetrated the hitherto exclusively Oxbridge domains of television, advertising and public relations. Hair lengthened, skirts
shortened and the sun came out over a Britain rejuvenated,
alert, and determined to have the best of times.[4]

Inhibitions were further relaxed by the Beatles' public
experimentation with drugs and their explorations, geo-
graphically and otherwise, into the worlds of mysticism and
eastern religions, and old convictions were sneered at by
those feeling the refreshing wind of liberation. Of course a
liberal approach wasn't really invented in the 60s any more
than sex itself; Bird and Hilborn point out that the generation born roughly between 1925–45, dubbed the Builder or
Silent generation, depending on which side of the Atlantic
they were born, was the generation that showed the biggest
ever age-bracket rise in the divorce rate as they reached
mid-life in the 70s; that the women of this generation were
chronologically the first mature female generation to take
the pill, and that, 'between the 1950s and the 1970s they
and their male peers reported the highest increase in sexual
intercourse of any previous generation in history'.[5]

It is not that no one had ever hinted at a sexuality smoul-
dering below the surface—take Marilyn Monroe and Elvis
Presley, born in 1926 and 1935 respectively, for example—
but that was as far as it went. Social norms in behaviour
were more or less observed across the board in this generation, thus keeping at bay anything that might seriously
threaten the status quo.

By the late 60s there was a little cloud on the horizon

called postmodernism. Foucault, Derrida and Leotard, the new existentialists, were publishing their ideas, and the West as a culture was beginning to realise that the answer to life's conundrums, toils and troubles did not lie in the economic prosperity or technological progress championed by the modernist era. It seemed clearer and clearer that the answer was that there wasn't an answer.

This meant that any answer could be an answer; indeed any answer was validated simply by being expressed, and so anyone could believe, think and act as he chose to without infringing commonly held absolutes.

> The 'Billy Graham years', spurred by the austerity, and socio-economic retrenchment that marked post-war reconstruction, and by a certain selflessness springing from these things, had yielded to the tidal wave of the sexual revolution, and by 1970 there had been a mass rejection of mainstream Christian faith and values, shown by a near 50% decline in church recruitment during the previous decade.[6]

The way was thus opened for an out and out race to be the most outrageous; and the last 25 years have seen a gradual but determined erosion of all the boundaries of once tacitly accepted modesty and decorum. So it is that we can read near-pornographic synopses of the latest film, be it about gang rape, sado-masochism or sexualised cannibalism, not in a magazine that we all recognise as adult literature because it is sealed in cellophane and up on the top shelf, but in the pages of our staid and respectable national newspapers. In the same way, the visual arts, from television to theatre, and the Internet have unlocked Pandora's box where sexuality is concerned, and we are a thoroughly sexualised society, where sex sells everything from cars to computers, and where children are forced to grow up before they've had a chance to enjoy childhood, too often becoming the sexual victims of their elders.

The prophet Isaiah, speaking to the apostate Judah in the eighth century BC says, 'Woe to those who call evil good, and good evil, who put darkness for light, and light for darkness, who put bitter for sweet and sweet for bitter.'[7]

Of course the old yardsticks against which to determine whether these things are happening have vanished, but the evidence is overwhelming, whether it is in the form of national statistics, such as the rising rate of teenage pregnancies and Chlamydia and STDs, or of personal experience.

In almost 25 years of ministry, I have found that the vast majority of emotional or psychological disturbances finds its roots in the sexual identity of the individual. That is to say, that a person suffering from nightmares, or another who consistently fails to make durable relationships, or a third who cannot escape compulsive behaviour, sexual or otherwise, is more than likely to have had their initial sexual encounter in a less than conducive context. Many have suffered abuse as a child or fled from demoralising or demeaning surroundings, such as violent or alcoholic parents, into the arms of someone who did not meet their need for comfort. It can take years to discover that love is not spelt s-e-x, and the pain and guilt are compounded with the passing of every one of those years.

The Old Testament story of Amnon and Tamar[8] illustrates the truth that sexual encounter outside God's design will so often breed hatred rather than love. Amnon was one of David's many sons. The story recounts that one day he fell in love with his half-sister. 'Amnon became frustrated to the point of illness on account of his sister Tamar, for she was a virgin, and it seemed impossible for him to do anything to her.' His friend Jonadab, described as a shrewd man, devises a ploy whereby Amnon can seduce Tamar. Feigning illness, he orders some lunch to be cooked and brought to him by her. Arriving with the food, Tamar finds herself not only suddenly alone with her brother, who has swiftly dismissed all his attendants, but instructed to feed him in the intimacy of his bedroom. 'But when she took it to him to eat, he grabbed her and said, "Come to bed with me my sister."' Not so ill after all, perhaps? Protesting vigorously, Tamar says such a thing would be not only wrong, but bring disgrace upon her, and tries to reason with Amnon, saying she is sure the king will allow them to marry if they ask. 'But he refused to listen to her, and since he was stronger than she, he raped her. Then Amnon hated her with intense hatred. In fact he hated her more than he had loved her. Amnon said to her, "Get up and get out!"' Deep fury is born in Absalom, Tamar's brother, also son to David, and two years later he murders Amnon in revenge for Tamar's disgrace and desolation. The story records, 'This has been Absalom's expressed intention ever since the day Amnon raped his sister Tamar.'[9]

Of all the many obstacles to being what God intended us to be and doing the things we were made to do, the idolatry and enslavement of sex, roaring like an escaped lion and seeking whom it may devour, as Peter describes the devil,[10] is surely one of the most fearful and successful. Its effects are seldom limited to what takes place between two individuals. Pregnancy, abortion, misery and broken relationships can follow; and as the story of David illustrates, sexual habits and practices often pass from one generation to another.

Certain individuals have been well aware of the power of sex and sought to exploit it under the guise of religious thought or the ideology of freedom. One such was Alice Bailey, the founder of the Theosophy Movement of the 1940s; a springboard for the religious smorgasbord that has come to be known as the New Age Movement.

In a plan, or mandate widely thought to have originated during the 1950s in the writings of Alice Bailey, ten strategies to promote a godless society, liberated from the restrictions of faiths in general and Christianity in particular, are outlined. I have seen several versions of this 'plan', but all have the same aims.

1. Take God out of school. Without reference to God he will become irrelevant.
2. Break the traditional Judaeo-Christian family concept. Discourage communication between parents and children about faith.
3. Remove restrictions on sex. Sex is man's greatest expression of enjoyment, and Christianity seeks to rob people of it.
4. Man must be free to enjoy any expression of sexuality. All forms of sexual expression are desirable so long as no one is being abused or harmed.
5. Work to provide abortion on demand. Women must be free to abort unwanted children.
6. Everyone develops 'soul-bonds'. Everyone should be free to follow his instincts, and marriage should be no

     obstacle to the creation of a new sexual relationship. Divorce must be readily available.

7. Defuse religious radicalism by silencing Christianity and promoting other faiths.

8. Use the media to influence mass opinion. Mould mass opinion to be receptive to these values.

9. Debase Art in all its forms, and make it obscene, immoral and occultic.

10. Endeavour to persuade the church to endorse these strategies, and to accept the principles enshrined in them.[11]

Little comment needs to be made on the way in which so much of this has become reality over the last 50 or so years.

But there is good news, and it is found at the cross where Jesus hung and died to make our sins as white as snow.[12] It is found in encountering the One who remembers our sins no more,[13] who sweeps away our offences like a cloud, our sins like the morning mist,[14] and says that he has removed our transgressions from us as far as the east is from the west.[15] This last picture used to make me worry that it would only take a day's plane travel to come upon the ghastly mountain of my sins and follies, and dread discovery and retribution, until I realised that the writer wasn't using the date line to calculate the distance between east and west!

Working for two years as part of the Living Waters team at our church in Paris, I saw many people set free from the chains of sexual addiction or pain that had caused them to walk with a limp for years or skewed their every attempt to build a fruitful life. I think of Polish Christina, a mature mother of two grown children, but long ago abandoned by their father. As the child of café owners serving long-distance lorry drivers, she had been used to serve them more than coffee, and this with the acquiescence of her parents. Slowly, in the safety of our small group of wounded women, we brought these haunting ghosts into the light, one by one. She spoke to Jesus of them, and listened to his Spirit until she heard the truth that she was not responsible for them, and the spell of the lie was for ever broken. There was no hurry, and there were many tears, not all of them shed by her, for the things we had to hear from one another were hard to bear. Today, Christina has remarried a gentle man called Thomas and her life has been rebuilt.

Don't let the spectre of past experiences in this realm anchor you to a place where you can only dream about destiny; where your heart cries out in recognition of deep calling to deep, but your body and your disappointed hopes and longings say no, not for you. That is a lie, and I encourage you, dear reader, to decide today that, like Christina, you will be free. The steps to gaining that freedom can only become clear once the decision is made.

PART 4

14

For You Created My Inmost Being

What is your destiny?

Turning the volume up, I raised my voice and accompanied Andrea Bocelli with abandon, singing at the top of my voice. The difference between us was that he was singing earthly love songs and I was singing heavenly ones. He sang to an audience of probably hundreds of thousands, and I was singing to an audience of one. Rain lashed the windscreen in the darkening air as I drove down the motorway, returning from a conference at which I had officially taken on a role within one of the numerous prayer networks around the world. It was a moment to remember and a journey of great joy. I was laughing and crying and singing and it had so much more to do with a brief and breathtaking glimpse of the big picture of my life than with the responsibility I had just taken on. Ha! So I did get to sing with somebody famous after all! It all depends on your perspective. . .

Postmodernism, the great answer to the failures of modernism, has done away with over-arching stories in which our own little individual stories have a place. There are no longer any absolute truths, so there are no signposts common to us all and by which we may find our way along life's road. The questioning of the necessity of the supernatural during the Enlightenment, perhaps a logical consequence of the Wars of Religion, was followed by Hume questioning the self-evident existence of God, Rousseau arguing for a society based on rights not responsibilities, and Kant proposing ethics deriving from human not divine sources. These things laid the foundations for today's deconstructionism, a 'pale Galilean Jesus and a distant God,'[1] and flung wide the door to usher in the god of humanism.

> The result is a belief in nothing, or perhaps more accurately, as G.K. Chesterton pointed out, a belief in everything. There is no over-arching truth that everyone must believe, yet the range of options of lifestyle choices and belief systems is dazzling, so that I can gaze at New Age crystals at the same time as working out in health and fitness clubs, arrange my home according to the principles of feng shui, go clubbing at nights and engage in Buddhist meditation when I wake up in the morning. Christianity takes its place among these as just another private life-style choice.[2]

But,

> In all of our hearts lies a longing for a sacred romance. It will not go away in spite of our efforts. . .to anaesthetise or ignore its song. . .it is a romance couched in mystery and set deeply within us. It cannot be categorised into propositional truths. . .any more than studying the anatomy of a corpse would help us know the person who once inhabited it.
>
> Philosophers call this romance, this heart-yearning, the longing for transcendence; the desire to be something larger

than ourselves, to be part of something out of the ordinary that is good.[3]

We know there is destiny.

Nearly always, when I am talking to or praying for someone, I encourage them to be 'seated in heavenly places'[4] with Jesus; in other words to try to look down on their circumstances rather than up from below them, and so regain perspective in a dark place or a foggy patch on the road. So often things are obscured from our understanding and we are tempted to give up. Another verse that is well worn in my Bible is, 'For anyone out there who doesn't know where you're going, anyone groping in the dark, here's what: Trust in God, Lean on your God!'[5] Same message; if you can't see don't worry, just switch on your fog lamps and proceed with caution. The road won't disappear, and there are still errands to run, things to drop off and people to pick up and give a lift to. We are all designed to be part of the coming of God's kingdom, to be men and women who carry the presence of Jesus, and who cause others to say, 'What is that perfume you're wearing?' Paul talks in these terms, and of course not everyone will like our perfume.

> But thanks be to God who leads us in triumphal procession in Christ and through us spreads everywhere the fragrance of the knowledge of him For we are to God the aroma of Christ among those who are being saved and those who are perishing. To the one we are the smell of death, to the other the fragrance of life. And who is equal to such a task?[6]

Not me! But to know God is to carry his presence. We see that some won't like it, but it's not the perfume that's off; the smell is perfect but it contains a message, the scent of a

far-off country, just as the smell of a rose or a lily can trans-
port us in an instant to the country of our childhood. For
some the message is the answer to the question they've
always been asking, but for others the message reacts with
the deceitfulness of the human heart, with anger, rage, mal-
ice, slander, greed, idolatry, immorality, impurity, unbelief or
any number of other gods that may control that particular
heart. And a powerful chemical stink arises. For yet others,
it's less clear: from the recesses of the corrupted heart there
rises the distant memory of a better smell, and it draws the
person to the aroma of Christ.

That's how it was for me.

Without being aware of it, Charlie and I first met at the
age of five at a beach picnic in west Wales, where our families had met while on holiday. Years later, I would learn that
this was a distressing period for his own parents who were
subsequently divorced; indeed, just after this event, when
holidays in Wales had become de rigueur for a number of
families, there was a rush of pubescent fervour, largely due
to the sudden and virtually simultaneous activation of
everyone's hormones, during which I found myself pursued
by Charlie, while at the same time completely deserted by
my appetite and intelligence, owing to an uncontrollable
passion for his cousin. So at that stage I was unimpressed by
his fireside conversation and his subtle attempts to put his
arm round me! Such is the confusion of the adolescent
world.

Four years later we found ourselves in the same city of
dreaming spires, where our relationship evolved from
friend to lover over a period of time, neither of us having
yet had an encounter with Christ, though we knew about

him. Charlie had made his way here to become a student at this ancient seat of learning, and I had fled here, envious of my friends, of whom he was by now one of the closest, and dissatisfied with the college where I had started my studies to become a teacher. At this college I had been approached by some students who said they were Christians, but far from drawing me by their winsomeness, they alarmed me with their dowdy clothes, thick stockings and severe hair styles. Paul says 'I have become all things to all men so that by all possible means I might save some.'[7] I don't think he meant that he would compromise his faith or principles in his desire to reach others, but rather that he would do his very best to find some common ground and gain a hearing. Legalism in any shape or form of course has the opposite effect. In any case, my heart was dry at the time, and I was not yet alive to the pulse of faith. I certainly didn't fancy the dress code it appeared to offer.

As a language student, Charlie was obliged to spend a year abroad, which meant a separation. This was something I dreaded, being by this time unhealthily dependent on the relationship that had developed between us. I think he probably saw the year as a welcome escape, though he would not have been able (or dared?) to articulate such a thought. The truth was that without boundaries or a firm foundation, our situation was cloying and claustrophobic and brought us very little satisfaction or happiness. We had frequent arguments and brief separations, and my pleadings were certainly counter-productive. All the same we limped on, and I made several visits to his rather austere little apartment in the Rue de Berne in Strasbourg. Occasionally since, if I found myself visiting a less than fragrant cabinet de toilette in Paris, a powerful memory of the Rue de Berne loo would sweep over me. These were the heydays of Bob Dylan and Leonard Cohen, and their mournful compositions suited us well. Despite an uneasy truce and our volatile existence together, we were making plans to cohabit once Charlie returned to Oxford for his final year. By now I was living in a potentially perfect flat right in the centre of the city, and it seemed obvious that we should share it when the time came.

The time did come, but it wasn't the time I thought. Another still in the memory file is of Charlie standing at the bottom of the stairs that led to the flat and saying, carefully and clearly, 'I don't really want to live with you any more. I'm too young, it's too soon.' Not for the first or last time in my life, my stomach performed an involuntary somersault as I searched for a reply. But as is so often the case, God was in this apparent catastrophe. My young man's decision was not up for discussion, and he'd clearly done some careful and conclusive thinking. So now I had to get my skates on and do some fast tap dancing if I was going to be able to transfer my place for post-graduate studies.

A hurried application led to an open door into a teacher training college that ironically had turned down my application some years earlier, and after a silent and almost ceremonious separating of all our personal effects, helped by my father, who was certainly most relieved by this development, I was on my way to Cambridge, a tormented muddle of thoughts and emotions, to begin a new life.

A new life was indeed exactly what awaited me, but I had no idea as yet just how new. A strange thing had happened in our God-fearing and upright family the previous year:

my younger sister had 'become a Christian'. What an absurd idea and arrogant claim! She already was a Christian of course, having been born into a good church-going Protestant family. Nevertheless, I was somewhat apprehensive of finding myself anywhere near a bunch of fanatics as I moved to the same city, though at the same time I craved security at any price. My father and I had often exchanged amused remarks with each other at my sister's expense, knowing of course that normality would return once the dust had settled. I was not only apprehensive of my present move, but almost perpetually on the edge of irritation; I had discovered that my sister and her friends prayed for me and was very put out by such cheek.

Something happened, however, which began to change my life before I was aware of it, and the change was to prove momentous. Having nowhere to live, I was taken in by three students who shared a tiny little house, yet were apparently willing for me to sleep in their minute sitting-room until I found accommodation. This in itself impressed me, but I was perhaps even more struck by the orderly lives led by these three sweet girls. Nothing could have provided more of a contrast with the lifestyle of my Oxford flat, where washing-up only took place if the kitchen was completely devoid of clean implements, and even then it was usually partial. Housework never took place. Parties were a regular event and an inordinate amount of alcohol was consumed. I can remember stumbling into the bathroom on many occasions and thinking as I threw up that this wasn't really what I enjoyed. Now, I was in a very clean place, in every sense of the word.

In the months that followed, I went through an intense

time of questioning and debate, sometimes with myself and often with one or other of the many Christ-followers, into whose orbit I had come, as if through the Narnian wardrobe. I still went to parties too and maintained the old lifestyle, afraid that too much exposure to my new friends would make me strange. I didn't hide my pain and confusion, however, nor the fact that I was intrigued if not captivated by the Christians. They were unfailingly patient with my untutored ways and unending questions. With one, I would sit until way into the small hours, chain-smoking cigarillos and pressing every question with intensity. All the time, the subject of the resurrection of Jesus, at first very faint and indistinct, loomed nearer and clearer, until one night I drifted off to sleep in my new-found accommodation, a student house much less inviting than my first port of call in Cambridge.

It was January 23rd, 1974. My room was suddenly, inexplicably and completely filled with what I knew to be the presence of God. It was thick, but didn't prevent me instantly sitting bolt upright, my heart crashing against my rib-cage, and then clambering from the bed to fall on my knees. 'All right, Lord,' I said, 'You win.' Not perhaps the most appropriate response to the King of kings, I realised with hindsight. But something so life-changing was taking place that searching for eloquence didn't cross my mind. Deep down, I knew that the months of debate and heart-searching and wrestling with apologetics (up to this moment in the role of devil's advocate) were reaching a climax and resolution; and I knew that from this day forward my life would never be the same; and that its direction would almost certainly radically change. I also knew that as far as I was concerned, the resurrection of Jesus was the central and most certain of all historical facts and, that being the case, it was to become the most central fact of my own life: and that had implications.

The first of these was to inform Charlie of my new-found status in life. We had remained in touch periodically, and had just come to the end of a self-imposed six-month moratorium on phone calls and long letters. So I sat down to write to him and describe the passage from cynicism to certainty; to urge him to read the enclosed copy of C. S. Lewis' *Mere Christianity* and go out, buy a Bible and read the four gospels at one sitting. Then we would review the situation. For by now, with the passing of time and the freedom of living without me, he was not so sure that he wanted the break to be definitive. Phone calls, discussions and heated debates ensued. Majestically awkward meetings between Charlie and my new-found friends were arranged by me in the first flush of excitement about Jesus. I manoeuvred and manipulated, all to no avail, and it was only when I grasped the truth that God alone could change his heart and let go with a certain relief that the lock was sprung. 'No one comes to the Father except through Me,' says Jesus.[8] 'Blessed are you. . .for this was not revealed to you by man, but by my Father in heaven.[9]

That's another story, which led in turn to our marriage and in due course to the birth of two daughters, and in 1981 our son Samuel. And so terribly soon afterwards to the greatest and most unexpected upheaval in our lives, when Samuel died a week after our arrival in California.

One year earlier, we had made arrangements to do Charlie's statutory second-year placement in the beautiful city of York, at a church rapidly becoming well-known in evangelical circles thanks to the ministry of a remarkable man, David Watson, then the vicar of St Michael-le-Belfry. David died of cancer in 1984 but already in 1981 the work that he and his wife Anne were doing was becoming known because of their radical devotion to the teaching of Jesus and their refusal to make religious compromises. They were hungry for more of God and were prepared to take the rough with the smooth. They had made a decision, at the time considered very avant-garde, to live, with their two young children, in community. That is to say, they took three or four students into the rambling and rather large vicarage and committed themselves to live as a family. Inevitably this was not without its tensions in a world which had long dispensed with such outmoded ideas, but nonetheless many doors opened up to David to teach and communicate the things he had been privileged to learn with his family and household.

Our Oxford days had found us fairly consistently mixing with the theatre crowd, and a character who had particularly struck us was an American called Geoffrey, a theology student at Keble. We were attracted by his quiet and cultivated air and warmed to his thoughtfulness. A firm friendship had been established and maintained; the years had passed; we had been invited to one another's marriages, and now Geoffrey lived in York with his wife and two small daughters. It was to their beautiful home in Bootham, near the city centre, that we came to learn from this vibrant church.

As young Christians, these were heady days. We had discovered Jesus; now we were discovering his church, and it is no exaggeration to say that we fell in love with her. We had both grown up in the traditional Anglican Church to one degree or another. Neither of us had had any idea that faith could be expressed in ways so much more immediate than those we had known to date. It was clearly going to be a good time from every point of view. It was a time that coincided with the birth in me of the desire for another child, and more specifically, a son. To begin with this was what might be expected during the period of establishing a new generation. However, I soon found myself devoting a disproportionate amount of time to this yearning and over-conscious of the normal cycle of hormonal fluctuations. Thinking myself pregnant, and certainly with a heightened spiritual awareness, I was distraught when bleeding began, and soon took an appointment with a doctor recommended by Geoffrey's wife, Judith.

To this day, I can recall my early morning walk to the surgery. It was a dismal winter day and the sky hung low over the city as it cranked into life again. Like the dense traffic, I hugged the city wall, blackened by centuries of dust and dirt and more recently by emissions of carbon dioxide. Equally clear is the doctor's verdict: 'Mrs Cleverly, although you had a positive pregnancy test, we are almost certain that your condition is not that of a normal pregnancy, but very probably a hydratidiform mole.'

A what?! My stomach was somersaulting, and I fought to control it as I asked the doctor, 'What do you mean?'

He carefully described a medical condition in which the egg is fertilised but simply begins a chaotic and formless multiplication of cells, therefore excluding any possibility of a normal pregnancy. He advised me to consult my GP on our return home to Bristol, as I would certainly require cleaning the womb in preparation for starting again. I walked slowly back beneath the black city wall with a despondent heart and a sinking stomach.

The following week was a special week at the church, called 'renewal week'. Word had spread far and wide over the years about the extraordinary life and liveliness that was to be found at St Michael's. The worship was exhilarating; David's preaching captivating and edifying; and, most intriguing of all, people testified to being healed when prayed for at the end of services; some prayed in the tongues of angels, and some seemed to faint with all the excitement—or was it really that? At any rate, the scene as the Sunday service drew to a close bore so little resemblance to what might loosely have been called Anglican that it inevitably attracted a great deal of attention, much of it from those who hungered after a relationship with God that had to date eluded them, and which they saw here was possible.

Renewal week was born to help meet this hunger and comprised all sorts of seminars, services and plenary sessions. Idly discussing this plethora of church activity, in which Charlie was fully implicated thanks to his placement, I felt suddenly that I must go to the healing service that was one of the week's focal points. Sitting in the crowded church beside a friend I listened as it was explained that all were welcome to go forward for prayer, but that it was not the time for explanations or counselling; only prayer. Although I had felt I must come to the service, I now felt persuaded that my needs were so insignificant compared to the vast majority of those present (in particular my friend who was currently undergoing tests for multiple sclerosis—this seemed so overwhelming and dramatic that my own fears shrank momentarily to almost nothing) that I decided to sit tight and watch; and pray.

'You must go forward.' The voice was almost audible and I turned round to see who had spoken, as I rose sheepishly from my seat to take my place in the queue that was inching forward to the altar. 'I so hope no one has seen me,' I thought. In those early days, it was still difficult to admit need publicly. I felt awkward and out of my comfort zone but was distracted from my self-consciousness by the need to plan for my arrival at the altar. It wouldn't do to be prayed for by a man, since my need was very personal. I couldn't tell a man that I was bleeding.

'I'd like to be prayed for by a woman,' I said firmly, praying that no questions would be asked. I was directed round the large altar rail and found myself at a space, looking into the kindly face of Anne Watson.

'My insides are in a mess and we'd like to have another baby,' I said lamely, and dropped to my knees. Anne began to pray, quite quietly and authoritatively. I don't remember all she said, but I remember that it was quite a long prayer and that, as she prayed, I felt the tension and anxiety drop away from me and a sense of peace settling on my shoulders like a comforting blanket. I also remember that about halfway through, her prayer became prophetic. At first praying for my consolation, she now began to speak of the son we would have and of how he would be a servant of the living God all the days of his life.

She drew to a close and, raising my head, my eyes met hers as she smiled, her expression full of tenderness. Turning, I made my way back to my seat, hope coursing through me like a mountain river leaping into life as snow yields to the warm caress of spring. Instinctively I knew that I had witnessed a real transaction in the spiritual world. Quite suddenly my anguished confusion had been transformed into certainty born of faith. I knew that I was experiencing grace and kindness from God. I was going to have a child and, what's more, a son who already had a calling.

Returning home elated, I recounted the service to Charlie, Geoffrey and Judith; omitting, however, that all this had left me with a new conviction, despite the doctor's solemn advice. Several weeks later, I was sitting in our GP's surgery in Bristol, explaining my condition and the need for a D&C. Dr Stanford was a kindly man with a keen sense of humour. He had once told me, when I was afflicted by a severe and persistent cough, that the only thing that would cure it was heroin and he wasn't allowed to prescribe that. On another occasion, awaiting the birth of Alice, and well past the appointed date of delivery when I made a routine visit to see him, he nodded his head in the direction of the mantelpiece, indicating the bottle of cod liver oil. 'A good dose of that would start you off,' he said. 'I made my wife take it every time. Marvellous stuff.'

Now he looked at me thoughtfully and there was quite a long pause before he answered. The pendulum clock ticked loudly and there was an expectant silence. My eyes roamed over the heavy antique furniture, anxious to avoid hurrying him with my stare.

'Hmm,' he said slowly. 'Well, I think we'll have a scan before we make any decisions.'

And so it was that some days later, this time in hospital, the radiologist said the unthinkable. 'You have a twelve-week foetus in there, and as far as I can see everything is perfectly normal.'

'Well,' I recognised Dr Stanford's avuncular tones as he entered the room, 'lucky we weren't too hasty, eh?'

Thus, as far as I was concerned, a miracle had happened and I was bearing a child known and called by God. His future was assured and his paths prepared by heaven. All of this served to consolidate in a remarkable way our relatively fledgling faith, and the dark days of winter gave way to a spring and summer of joy and laughter as my belly slowly swelled and we awaited the arrival of Samuel, already named because, like Hannah, I had asked the Lord for him. When Samuel died we had to start all over again, but for now our time for trial had not yet come and wrestling with this issue lay ahead of us.

Every child has a potentially assured future and his paths mapped out by heaven. Every child is designed and known by God.

> For you created my inmost being; you knit me together in my mother's womb. I praise you because I am fearfully and won-derfully made. . .My frame was not hidden from you when I was made in the secret place. When I was woven together in the depths of the earth, your eyes saw my unformed body. All the days ordained for me were written in your book before one of them came to be.[10]

You can't get much clearer than that. So why are the ordained days of so many cut short? At the beginning of the twenty-first century, the world is watching many lives being cut short as accident, war and natural disasters fall upon the earth and its inhabitants day after day. Why an omnipotent God permits these things is the very crux of the ancient dilemma of suffering. It is not my purpose to attempt an answer to this question; it lies in the realms of theology and philosophy that are far beyond my scope or ability, if indeed it can be answered at all this side of heaven.

My purpose throughout this book has been to call you to live well through such life-changing storms; to set a steady course through the turbulence and to make it through. At all costs, find out what you were made to do and do it. Whether you are a teenager, a student, an Xer, a parent or a grandparent—whatever your age today—lift up your eyes to the presence and power of God at work all over the world. Don't be satisfied with a report of this from the media or textbooks. The real news has always been bypassed or simply suppressed.

We own a book called *Oxford in the History of the Nation*, which makes no mention of three of the most glorious martyrs England has ever known. It is silent about Cranmer, Latimer and Ridley, all of whom gave up their lives for the sake of Jesus as they were burnt at the stake outside Trinity College in this city.

Be hungry to know God and to live for him, and perhaps die for him. Search out and read the stories of those who have decided to go wholeheartedly for the call of Christ: martyrs of every century and every nation.[11] Remember that more people are giving their lives for Christ now than at any other period of history. Seek out the company of like-minded souls: 'Do not be misled: bad company corrupts good character.'[12] To quote one of my favourite verses: 'Do everything without complaining or arguing, so that you may become blameless and pure, children of God without fault in a crooked and depraved generation, in which you shine like stars in the universe as you hold out the word of life. . .'[13] Don't let your personal story obscure the grand story in which you have a unique role. Are you worried about who you will marry? The Lord of the universe is more than able to match you with a partner who will be your earthly companion and lover in the big story to which you are called, which is the establishing of the lordship of Jesus Christ. Paul puts it like this: 'God's will, which he long ago planned to accomplish through the coming to earth of Jesus, is to bring all things in heaven and on earth together under Him.' You have a place in this, and whether you find the fullness of life that Jesus said he came to earth to give us depends on whether you decide that following him, whatever that may mean, now or in the future, is far and away your greatest and most glorious priority.

If like me you have passed out of the comforting confines of Generation X as I have, take heed. Statistics point overwhelmingly to faith being found in the first half of life. The mind is more open, courage is intact, possibilities are infinite. Later on disappointment has a hold; the notion of destiny has faded.

'I'm the King of Salem,' the old man had said.

'Why would a king be talking with a shepherd?' the boy asked, awed and embarrassed.

'For several reasons, but let's say that the most important is that you've succeeded in discovering your destiny.'

The boy didn't know what a person's destiny was.

'It's what you have always wanted to accomplish. Everyone, when they are young, knows what their destiny is.

'At that point in their lives everything is clear and everything is possible. They are not afraid to dream and to yearn for everything they would like to see happen to them in their lives. But, as time passes, a mysterious force begins to convince them that it will be impossible for them to realize their destiny.'[14]

Energy declines, horizons draw close, ambitions shrink and we are tempted to simply live out our days as best and as comfortably as possible. I urge you to listen to your children and your grandchildren. They know money can't buy them love; they know that nation rises against nation and kingdom against kingdom. They see famines, earthquakes and war.[15] They see that the love of many is growing cold. They see the advance of the European Union and they understand the consequent diminishing of freedom. They understand that the perpetual conflict in the Middle East has more to do with ancient tribal tension than seeking settlement, with spiritual forces than political negotiation. They understand that many have chosen to serve mammon rather than God, because the returns are quicker and more gratifying. They know that the time to choose is here.

And it is never too late; the pages of the Bible are strewn with stories of the elderly: Abraham, Moses, Jacob, Zechariah, Elizabeth, Simeon, Anna. . .

Tom and Joan Beak were over 70 when the Lord spoke to them and told them they were to start—yes, start!—a ministry in Togo. They didn't even know where Togo was and had to find an atlas. But just like Abraham, they obeyed, they found Togo and went there, and today the 'Ministry of Jesus' is flourishing.[16] Indomitable, Tom and Joan moved on; to retire, as would be proper at their age? Not a bit of it. They ventured off in the opposite direction and purchased a 420 acre farm about an hour away from Quito in Ecuador! Curiously, I heard from them as I was putting the finishing touches to the manuscript for this book. Now aged 89 and 84 respectively, they had completed their second project in 2005, the erection of a training and retreat centre on the farm called The Meeting Place. And they were on the move again: '. . .we expect to leave the house fully furnished, and take away only our personal things, books , family mirrors and silver etc., so we will be starting again from scratch.' The Lord, they say, hasn't finished with them yet! 'He says we can have a vacation and then he has other work for us to do. What can one say? Only Yes, Lord!'

Such stories should shake us free from slumber and apathy.

As a baby boomer born in the post-war generation that threw off the traces of the discipline necessarily imposed by war, I write with a deep conviction that, together with other boomers, I need to ask forgiveness of our children. I am part of a generation that popularised sex, if one may so express it; a generation that approved divorce and abortion; a generation that revolted against ancient boundaries; and the consequences of all these things are being reaped by the next generation—our children.

Yes, I was influenced by the philosophers of my time. At the tender age of 17, I spent a year in France, discovering the amazing psychedelic reaches of Sartre, Camus and company, as I took a philosophy course. I remember an extraordinary boat trip across Lake Victoria, taken the following summer with some friends during the four years my parents spent working in a school in Uganda. My back propped against the deck, my flesh basking in the sun's warmth, and my spirit delighting in the wide horizon of my future, I devoured *The Second Sex*, principal work of Simone de Beauvoir, the existentialist and long-term lover of Sartre. Like a sponge I drank in what I took to be the key to understanding as she traced the development of male oppression through historical, literary and mythical sources, attributing its contemporary effects on women to, 'the systematic objectification of the male as a positive norm'. 'Yes, I agree!' I thought, and decided under an African sky to be her disciple. Unbeknown to me at that rather pompous moment, the God who formed me in my mother's womb had other plans.

Paul says that, 14 years before he wrote the Second Letter to the Corinthians, he had an experience of God that he was not permitted to tell.[17] In 1990, I was in Switzerland at a conference that had gathered some 300 people. At the close of one of his talks, the speaker said, 'There's someone here called Anita,' and once I had identified myself (with what must have seemed to him a frustrating delay; I was sure there must be someone else present called Anita!), he continued by speaking of difficulties that lay ahead of me but would not overcome me. During that same conference I had what seemed to me a sobering glimpse into the future concerning persecution that, like Paul, I have never been able to speak of in detail. At the close of one evening we were requested to remain silent as we returned to our rooms for the night. Filing out of the hall a powerful vision that I have never forgotten came to me. It had to do with persecution in Europe becoming as real as it is in Iraq, the Sudan or Pakistan. Only time will tell if my vision was accurate. But I knew from that moment on that, good or bad, easy or difficult, my destiny was bound securely up with Christ and that nothing would ever deter me from following him, whatever it cost.

What about you? The choice is yours: will you respond to the dangerous but exhilarating invitation that God makes you and I? I invite you to choose to be a child of destiny, whether you are 18 or 80.

In the meantime, as I leave you to consider this, thank you for coming with me along this road with a view of eternity. Remember that the most important ingredient of destiny is love, and that to be an unsung hero like my father, who died during the completion of this manuscript, and who knew how to love, is a reward that exceeds our greatest achievement and our deepest longing.

Epilogue

It was January 23rd, 2005. 'Would Hannah make us grandparents today?' I wondered, musing on how poetic that would be. We had been on edge, with the inexperience of first-time grandparents, since the due date more than a week ago. But it was not to be. However, the delay provided me with some extra time to complete my manuscript, and I typed away waiting for the telephone beside me to ring. Day succeeded day, and item after item was crossed off my 'to do' list. On January 29th a phone call informed us that labour had begun, but like many first timers, it proved to be long and exhausting, and more nail-biting waiting ensued. I kept writing and writing, and towards the end of the morning triumphantly banged my finger down on the final full stop. I really had completed my first book! (First draft!) The exhilaration was dizzying.

Reuben Samuel made his equally dizzying appearance early in the afternoon, and thus the first member of the next generation in our family, a new child of destiny, was born on the same day as this book.

One day I will tell him that his grandmother had a baby on the same day that he was born. . .but for now I must record the greatest of all acknowledgements; to the Father, from whom his whole family in heaven and on earth derives its name.

Deo Gracias.

Anita Cleverly
Oxford 2005

Endnotes

Chapter 1: Unless a Seed Fall to the Ground

1. 2 Corinthians 5:1
2. 1 Corinthians 15:42–44
3. Romans 8:38,39
4. W. B. Yeats
5. Matthew 27:46

Chapter 2: Double Blessing

1. Isaiah 40:30,31
2. Psalm 91:2
3. Job 19:5,6
4. 1 Corinthians 15:20
5. 1 Corinthians 15:54

Chapter 3: Made to Measure

1. Simon Guillebaud, Newsletter, November 2003
2. Mike Bickle, *The Pleasures of Loving God* (Charisma House, 2000)
3. *Open Heavens* Vol 1. CD produced by Wesley and Stacey Campbell, 2003
4. by Pete Greig and Dave Roberts (Kingsway, 2003)
5. *Ibid* pp. 13–14
6. *Ibid* pp. 60–62
7. The full version of this prophetic word is published at www.worldtrumpetmission.org
8. Matthew 2:2
9. Douglas Coupland, *Life After God* (Simon & Schuster, 1999)

10. Ezekiel 4:16,17
11. Ecclesiastes 3:11
12. Galatians 4:4,5
13. Matthew 16
14. Luke 22

Chapter 4: The Hearts of the Fathers

1. Carol Wimber, *John Wimber:The Way It Was* (Hodder, 1999)
2. Titus 1:4
3. 1 Timothy 1:2,18
4. Galatians 4:19
5. 2 Corinthians 6:11,13
6. Lydia Fellowship International, a women's prayer network, founded in 1970
7. Isaiah 49:15
8. John Humphrys, *Devil's Advocate* (Random House, 1999)
9. Douglas Coupland, *Generation X* (Abacus, 1996) pp. 25–26
10. Malachi 4:6
11. Deuteronomy 6:6–9
12. What Would Jesus Do?
13. Psalm 141:3
14. Ephesians 4:32
15. Psalm 78:1–7 *The Message*
16. Psalm 22:30,31
17. 1 Timothy 4:12
18. *Ibid* v.14
19. 2 Timothy 1:5 *The Message*
20. Proverbs 1:1–4 *The Message*
21. Scottish Syllabus for Sex Education, 2004
22. *The State of our Nation*, Maranatha Community, December 2004
23. DoH 2002
24. NSPCC Child Protection Helpline, 2003
25. Children's Society, 2001
26. Institute for Alcohol Studies, 2004; ACMD, 2003

27. Home Office R&D Statistics Division, March 2004
28. Social Trends 33, 2004, ONS
29. Nuffield Research Project, September 2003
30. BBC survey of 50 A&E departments, August 2003
31. Shelter, 2004
32. Isaiah 54:1
33. Ephesians 4:13–15 *The Message*

Chapter 5: Simeons and Samuels, Hannahs and Annas

1. Charlie Cleverly, *The Discipline of Intimacy* (Kingsway, 2002)
2. C. S. Lewis, *The Screwtape Letters* (Harper Collins, 2002)
3. 1 Samuel 1: 9
4. Hebrews 5:7
5. In E. M. Bounds, *A Treasury of Prayer* (Bethany House, 1961)
6. 1 Samuel 1:17
7. Luke 1:45
8. 2 Chronicles 16:9
9. Rob Parsons, *Bringing Home the Prodigals* (Hodder, 2003)

Chapter 6: Slowing Down and Sweetening Up

1. Henri Nouwen, *Seeds of Hope* (DLT, 1993) p. 6
2. Ephesians 2:10
3. Philippians 3:12
4. 1 Samuel 16
5. 1 Samuel 20:42
6. Proverbs 27:6
7. Ephesians 4:15
8. Jehoshaphat's prayer, 2 Chronicles 20:7; James 2:23
9. Genesis 18:17
10. 2 Chronicles 20:7; Isaiah 41:8; James 2:23
11. Exodus 33:11
12. Matthew 6:22,23
13. Amos 3:7
14. Matthew 23:37
15. John 15:15

16. John 15:12–14
17. Romans 11:33
18. Acts 16:13–15

Chapter 7: A Church for All Nations

1. Revelation 7:9
2. Revelation 1:11
3. *Let the Sea Resound.* Video produced by the Sentinel Group (George Otis, 2004)
4. Introduction, P. Dixon, *Futurewise* (Profile Books, 2003)
5. Matthew 8:20b
6. Luke 9:24
7. *Futurewise.* p. 149
8. 2 Corinthians 2:14
9. Brother Yun, *The Heavenly Man* (Monarch, 2002)
10. Revelation 2:5
11. Bill Hybels, *Courageous Leadership* (Zondervan, 2002)

Chapter 8: All You Need Is Love

1. 1 Corinthians 13:1–3
2. Ezekiel 16
3. Therese de Lisieux autobiography (Doubleday, 1957)
4. Jim Elliot. For more see www.intouch.org
5. See Chapter 3
6. Rick Joyner, *Count Zinzendorf and the Hidden Seed of the Harvest*
7. Psalm 63:1
8. Their story is told in *There is Always Enough* (Sovereign World, 2003)
9. Matthew 5:11,12 *The Message*
10. Matthew 8:20
11. Matthew 19:16ff
12. 1 Corinthians 8:1
13. Philippians 3:4–6
14. 2 Corinthians 12:2–4
15. 2 Corinthians 6:5

16. Philippians 1:21
17. Acts 28:16,23

Chapter 9: Making Poverty History

1. Isaiah 58:6,7,10
2. Michele Guinness, *Woman, the Full Story* (Zondervan, 2003)
3. Josephine's letter to her sister Harriet, April 1883, quoted in *Glen Petrie, A Singular Iniquity* (Macmillan, 1971)
4. Fully recounted in *Woman, the Full Story* (Zondervan, 2003)
5. Joan Johnson, *James and Mary Ellis* (Historical Committee of the Religious Society of Friends in Ireland, 2000)
6. *Ibid*
7. Esther 4:12–14
8. James and Mary Ellis
9. *Ibid*
10. *Ibid*
11. Brycchan Carey, *William Wilberforce's Sentimental Rhetoric: Parliamentary Reportage and the Abolition Speech of 1789*
12. Michele Guinness, *Woman, the Full Story* (Zondervan, 2003)
13. Luke 10:25ff
14. Proverbs 14:31
15. James 2:17 & 1:22
16. UNAIDS
17. UNICEF
18. International Labour Organisation
19. Action International
20. For more information visit the website: www.arocha.org
21. Aldates Community Transformation Initiatives
22. Patrick Macdonald, *Reaching Children in Need* (Kingsway, 2000)

Chapter 10: God's Retirement Plan Is Out of this World

1. Dylan Thomas, 'Do not go gentle into that good night'
2. C. S. Lewis, *The Business of Heaven* (Fount, 1984)
3. Augustine

4. John Donne

5. John Bunyan

6. John Mulinde, founder and leader of Trumpet Mission, Uganda

7. Psalm 42:7

8. C. S. Lewis, *Four Loves* (Fount, 1977)

9. Isaiah 51:6

10. 1 Kings 8:27

11. Psalm 103:11

12. Isaiah 55:8

13. 1 Kings 8:30

14. Isaiah 66:1

15. Genesis 28:12,13

16. Exodus 20:22

17. Genesis 28:13,14

18. 2 Chronicles 7:14

19. Exodus 16:4

20. Matthew 19:14

21. Matthew 18:3,4

22. Ezekiel 1:1

23. Philip Pullman, *The Amber Spyglass* (Scholastic Press, 2001)

24. Hebrews 12:18

25. Isaiah 6

26. 2 Chronicles 5;13,14

27. Joshua 5:14

28. Acts 26:19

29. Acts 7:54–56

30. Mark Stibbe, *Fire and Blood* (Monarch, 2001)

31. Philippians 3:20

32. Dwight Moody

33. John 17:3

34. 1 Corinthians 15:42,43,53

35. Job 22:30 *The Message*

36. C. S. Lewis, *The Problem of Pain* (Fount, 1977)

Chapter 11: Goaded By Guilt

1. Ravi Zacharias, *Cries of the Heart* (Word Publishing, 1998)
2. BBC Radio 4; bbc.co.uk; *The Independent*; *The Telegraph*
3. Article 214 of 'Stephen's Digest of the Criminal Law', (thed; 1950). Confirmed by Lord Scarman, 1979, and the European Court of Human Rights, 1996
4. 1 Samuel 15:22,23
5. 1 Samuel 15:28
6. Genesis 25–35
7. Karl Barth
8. Luke 7:36–50
9. Dag Hammarskjold

Chapter 12: Untimely Death

1. Jeremiah 1:5
2. Psalm 139:16
3. Philippians 1:21–24
4. 1 Corinthians 13:3
5. Ephesians 4:13
6. Michael was born in 1994
7. Philippians 2:3
8. Angela Beise, 2003
9. John 10:10
10. Hebrews 11:16

Chapter 13: A Loaf of Bread

1. Visit www.alpha.org for details
2. 1 Corinthians 6:13,15,16
3. Philip Larkin, *Annus Mirabilis* (1974)
4. Ian MacDonald, *Revolution in the Head* (Pimlico, 1998)
5. Bird & Hilborn, *God and the Generations* (Paternoster, 2002)
6. *Ibid*
7. Isaiah 5:20
8. 2 Samuel 13
9. The whole story is found in 2 Samuel 13 and 14

10. 1 Peter 5:8
11. Adapted from Mark Stibbe's account of a message preached by John Mulinde in 1999
12. Isaiah 1:18
13. Isaiah 43 :25
14. Isaiah 44 :22
15. Psalm 103:12

Chapter 14: For You Created my Inmost Being

1. Graham Tomlin, *The Provocative Church* (SPCK, 2002)
2. *Ibid* p. 18
3. John Eldredge, *The Sacred Romance* (Nelson, 1997) p. 19
4. Ephesians 2:6
5. Isaiah 50:10 *The Message*
6. 2 Corinthians 2:14–16
7. 1 Corinthians 9:22
8. John 14:6
9. Matthew 16:17
10. Psalm 139:13–16
11. See Charlie Cleverly, *The Passion that Shapes Nations* (Kingsway, 2005)
12. 1 Corinthians 15:33
13. Philippians 2:14–16
14. Paulo Coelho, *The Alchemist* (Harper Collins, 1999) p. 22
15. Matthew 24:6,7
16. For more on this story, see Chapter 7
17. 2 Corinthians 12:4